Perennials *for* Ontario

Alison Beck
Kathy Renwald

Principal photography by Tim Matheson

The Publisher: Lone Pine Publishing

10145 – 81 Avenue
Edmonton, AB T6E 1W9
Canada

1808 B Street NW, Suite 140
Auburn, WA
USA 98001

Website: http://www.lonepinepublishing.com

Canadian Cataloguing in Publication Data

Beck, Alison, 1971–
  Perennials for Ontario

Includes index.
ISBN 1-55105-262-8

1. Perennials—Ontario. I. Renwald, Kathy, 1951– II. Title.
SB434.B419 2001   635.9'32'09713   C00-911262-6

Editorial Director: Nancy Foulds
Project Editor: Shelagh Kubish
Editorial: Shelagh Kubish, Dawn Loewen
Illustrations Coordinator: Carol Woo
Photo Editor: Don Williamson
Research Assistant: Allison Penko
Production Manager: Jody Reekie
Book Design: Heather Markham
Cover Design: Robert Weidemann
Layout & Production: Monica Triska, Heather Markham, Elliot Engley
Image Editing: Elliot Engley, Arlana Hale-Anderson, Ian Dawe, Monica Triska, Heather Markham

Photography: all photographs are by Tim Matheson (with field identification by Dawna Ehman) or Tamara Eder, except Peter Thompstone 115a, 170, 171b, 181b, 183a, 183b, 184a, 187b, 191, 209, 211b, 224, 248, 249a, 250b, 251, 253a, 258, 261a, 261b, 314, 315b, 324, 325a, 326; David McDonald 117, 148, 245b; Karen Carriere 118, 119a, 141b, 142a, 143a, 143b, 149, 291, 292, 293, 327b; Horticolor ©2000 Nova-Photo-Graphik/Horticolor™ 119b, 131b, 151, 282b, 296, 297a, 297b, 327a; Janet Davis 290; Joan de Grey 130, 131a, 150, 264, 265a, 265b; Allison Penko 323b, Erika Markham, 45; Elliot Engley, 43.

Cover Photographs (from left to right) by Tim Matheson, bleeding heart, Michaelmas daisy, black-eyed Susan, daylily, hardy geranium, bellflower; *by Tamara Eder,* columbine

Back cover author photos: Alison Beck by Alan Bibby, Kathy Renwald by Tim Leyes

Bug Illustrations: Ian Sheldon

We acknowledge the financial support of the Government of Canada through the Book Publishing Industry Development Program (BPIDP) for our publishing activities.

PC: P1

CONTENTS

4

ACKNOWLEDGEMENTS

We express our appreciation to all who were involved in this project. Special thanks are extended to the following organizations and individuals: in Hamilton to the Royal Botanical Gardens; in Niagara to the Niagara Parks Commission; in St. Catharines to the Niagara College Horticulture Program; in Newington to Centre Commons Perennials.

Thanks also to Tim Matheson, Dawna Ehman, Peggy Coulter, Robin and Nancy Matheson, Barbara Matheson; in Vancouver to Acadia Community Garden at UBC, Michael Levenson and the Compost Demonstration Garden, Maple Leaf Nurseries, Pension Fund Realty Ltd. at Park and Tilford Gardens, Odessa Bromeley and Southside Perennials, Board of Parks and Recreation, Southland Nursery, Strathcona Community Gardens, UBC Botanical Gardens, VanDusen Gardens, West Van Florist, Westrend Gardening; in Victoria to Butchart Gardens; in Rosedale to Minter Gardens; in Edmonton to the Devonian Botanical Gardens, Alex and Bonnie Rosato, Ernst Eder, Heather Markham, Leslie Knight, Vladimir Salyzyn.

Additional thanks to Peter Thompstone for his generous contribution and involvement in preparing this book.

THE FLOWERS AT A GLANCE

Pictorial Guide in Alphabetical Order, by Common Name

Ajuga
p. 68

Anemone
p. 72

Artemisia
p. 76

Aster
p. 80

Astilbe
p. 84

Balloon Flower
p. 88

Basket-of-Gold
p. 90

Beard Tongue
p. 94

Bellflower
p. 98

Bergamot
p. 102

Bergenia
p. 106

Black-Eyed Susan
p. 110

Blazing Star
p. 112

Bleeding Heart
p. 114

Butterfly Weed
p. 118

Candytuft
p. 120

Cardinal Flower
p. 122

Catmint
p. 126

Christmas Rose
p. 130

Columbine
p. 132

Coneflower
p. 136

Coral Bells
p. 140

Coreopsis
p. 144

Corydalis
p. 148

Cupid's Dart
p. 150

Daylily
p. 152

Dead Nettle
p. 156

Delphinium
p. 160

Doronicum
p. 164

English Daisy
p. 166

Euphorbia
p. 168

Evening Primrose
p. 170

False Dragonhead
p. 172

False Rockcress
p. 174

False Solomon's Seal
p. 178

Foamflower
p. 180

Foxglove p. 182	**Geum** p. 186	**Goat's Beard** p. 188	**Goutweed** p. 192
Hardy Geranium p. 194	**Hens and Chicks** p. 198	**Hollyhock** p. 200	**Hosta** p. 204
Iris p. 208	**Jacob's Ladder** p. 212	**Lady's Mantle** p. 214	**Lamb's Ears** p. 218
Ligularia p. 220	**Lily-of-the-Valley** p. 224	**Lungwort** p. 228	**Lupine** p. 232
Lychnis p. 236	**Mallow** p. 238	**Marguerite Daisy** p. 242	**Meadow Rue** p. 244

Meadowsweet
p. 248

Monkshood
p. 252

Mullein
p. 256

Oriental Poppy
p. 258

Pachysandra
p. 262

Pasque Flower
p. 264

Peony
p. 266

Phlox
p. 270

Pincushion Flower
p. 274

Pinks
p. 276

Potentilla
p. 280

Primrose
p. 284

Red-Hot Poker
p. 288

Rose-Mallow
p. 290

Russian Sage
p. 294

Sandwort
p. 296

Sedum
p. 298

Shasta Daisy
p. 302

Snow-in-Summer
p. 304

Soapwort
p. 306

Speedwell
p. 308

Sweet Woodruff
p. 310

Tansy
p. 312

Thrift
p. 314

Thyme
p. 316

Vinca
p. 320

Violet
p. 322

Wall Rockcress
p. 324

Wild Ginger
p. 326

Yarrow
p. 328

Introduction

Perennials are plants that take three or more years to complete their life cycle. This is a broad definition that includes trees and shrubs. To narrow the definition in the garden we refer to herbaceous (non-woody) perennials as perennials. Herbaceous perennials live for three or more years, but they generally die back to the ground at the end of the growing season and start fresh with new shoots each spring. Some plants grouped with perennials do not die back completely—for example subshrubs such as thyme. Still others—evergreen perennials such as pinks—remain green all winter.

The temperate climate of Ontario, with its warm summers, cold winters and fairly dependable rainfall, is ideal for growing a wide range of perennials. Though the climate of all of Ontario is considered temperate, there is a great deal of diversity within this area. In general, cold Ontario winters provide ample dormancy for the perennials, such as peonies, to set flowers for the following summer. Summers range from fairly short in the north to long in the south, giving plants in the most populated southern parts of Ontario ample time to flourish. Summer weather in Ontario is classified as cool when compared to the far south of the United States, but can be hot and humid as far as garden plants are concerned. Winter conditions vary widely across Ontario, providing unique challenges in every garden. No matter how challenging the site, there are perennials that will flourish and provide the gardener with an almost limitless selection of colours, sizes and forms. This versatility, along with the beauty and permanence of perennials, lies at the root of the continued and growing popularity of perennials.

The far north of the province, bordering Hudson Bay and James Bay, is an area of lakes, muskeg, boreal forest and tundra. This sparsely populated area is for the most part accessible only by air, with few roads. Moving south towards Lake Superior, the terrain changes very little, but the climate becomes more habitable and more conducive to gardening. Cold winters bring plenty of protective snowcover, and many perennials can be grown here. The limiting factor is not the cold winter but the short growing season. Plants listed in this book as **hardy** will survive in this region.

East of Lake Superior, the central parts of Ontario contain more urban centres and a corresponding increase in population. South of the region, stretching from Sault Ste. Marie east to Sudbury and North Bay then skirting the southern edge of Algonquin Park and back up to Pembroke, a climate change opens up new possibilities for gardeners. This area benefits from the moderating influence of the Great Lakes on the cold arctic air that streams down in winter. The plants classified in this book as **semi-hardy** will survive in this region, even with minimal winter protection. Consistent protective snowcover and a longer

frost-free period in summer provide good conditions for perennials. Because perennials leave little, if any, live growth exposed above ground in the winter, the ice storms common to this area do not hurt perennials.

Warmer winter weather is experienced south of Guelph, Barrie, Peterborough and Ottawa, along with a much increased population density. As you move south of these cities, there is a change in the winter weather. The temperatures are not as cold and there is less likelihood of consistent snowcover. The fluctuations in winter temperatures create a series of freeze and thaw cycles that can be stressful to plants. A gardener in Ottawa, north of this area, may have more luck with some of the semi-hardy or tender plants than a gardener in much warmer Kitchener. Even so, the perennials classified as **tender** in this book can be expected to survive in this region. Using mulch will protect tender perennials from freeze and thaw cycles in winter.

Some of the warmest growing conditions in Canada occur in the Niagara Peninsula and at the very southern tip of Ontario around Windsor. On a latitude equal to that of the northern Mediterranean Sea, much of this warm growing region has been devoted to fruit and wine production.

There is more to growing perennials in Ontario than climate. The great diversity in soil types and growing conditions is a lesson in the varied geology of the province. The north and east of the province rests on the Canadian Shield. Here rock gardens and rock walls are always in style, often by necessity. The soil itself may consist of clay or sand and is often quite acidic. In contrast, gardeners living near the limestone-rich Niagara Escarpment work with alkaline soils. Marked all over with fertile river valleys and floodplains, Ontario provides one of the most interesting, challenging and rewarding places to create a perennial garden.

Don't feel too limited by information on large-scale climate zones, perennial hardiness and soil patterns. Microclimates abound, giving gardeners almost anywhere in Ontario the possibility of growing that one perennial that everyone says won't grow here. The challenge of gardening with plants that are borderline hardy is part of the fun of growing perennials. The proximity of buildings, how quickly the soil drains and whether you garden in a low, cold hollow or on top of a windswept knoll or hillside affect the microclimate of your own garden.

Outstanding garden shows, public gardens, arboretums and show gardens in Ottawa, Toronto, Hamilton, Guelph and Niagara Falls attract gardeners and growers from all over the world and are sources of inspiration as well as information. Unlike trees and shrubs, perennials are relatively inexpensive and easy to share with friends and neighbours, so the more varieties you try, the more likely you'll be to discover what loves to grow in your garden. When it comes to perennials, the best advice is to dig in and 'just grow for it.'

There are many enthusiastic and creative people involved in gardening in Ontario. From one end of the province to the other, individuals, growers, breeders, societies, schools, publications and public gardens provide information, encouragement and fruitful debate for the gardener. Ontario gardeners nurture a knowledge of planting and propagation methods, a precision in identifying specific plants, and a plethora of passionate opinions on what is best for any little patch of ground.

Average Annual
Minimum Temperature

NORTHERN   –34° C (–30° F) or colder

CENTRAL   –25° to –34° C (–15° to –30° F)

SOUTHERN   –18° to –25° C (0° to -15° F)

PERENNIAL GARDENS

*P*erennials can be used alone in a garden or combined with other plants. Perennials form a bridge between the permanent structure provided by trees and shrubs and the temporary colour provided by annuals. They often flower longer and grow to mature size more quickly than shrubs do and in many cases require less care and are less prone to pests and diseases than annuals are.

Perennials can be included in any size or style of garden. From the riot of colour in a cottage garden or the cool, soothing shades of green in a woodland garden, to a welcoming cluster of pots on a doorstep, perennials open up a world of design possibilities for even the inexperienced gardener.

It is very important when planning your garden to decide what you like. If you enjoy the plants that are in your garden, then you are more likely to take proper care of them. Decide what style of garden you like as well as what plants you like. Think about the gardens you have most admired in your neighbourhood, in books or while visiting friends. Use these ideas as starting points for planning your own garden.

A good perennial garden can be interesting throughout the year. Consider the foliage of the perennials you want to use. Foliage can be bold or flimsy, coarse or refined; it can be big or small, light or dark; its colour can vary from yellow, grey, blue or purple to any multitude of greens; and it can be striped, splashed, edged, dotted or mottled. The texture can be shiny,

Variety of textures

Next, consider the size and shape of different perennials. Choose a variety of forms to make your garden more interesting. The size of your garden influences these decisions, but do not limit a small garden to small perennials or a large garden to large perennials. Use a balanced combination of plant sizes that are in scale with their specific location. (See Quick Reference Chart, p. 332.)

Consider the colours of the flowers and the foliage of different perennials. Colours affect our senses. Cool colours, such as blue, purple and green, are soothing and make small spaces seem bigger. Warm colours, such as red, orange and yellow, are more stimulating and appear to fill large spaces. (See Quick Reference Chart, p. 332.)

Textures can also create a sense of space; some gardens are designed solely by texture. Larger leaves are considered coarse in texture and the fact that they are visible from a greater distance make spaces seem smaller and more shaded. Small leaves, or those that are finely divided, are considered fine in texture and create a sense of greater space and light.

fuzzy, silky, rough or smooth. The famous white gardens at Sissinghurst, England, were designed to remove the distraction of colour and allow the eye to linger on the foliage to appreciate its subtle appeal. Flowers come and go, but a garden planned with careful attention to foliage will always be interesting.

Select perennials that flower at different times in order to have some part of your garden flowering all season. (See Quick Reference Chart, p. 332.)

Decide how much time you will have to devote to your garden. With good planning and advanced preparation you can enjoy low-maintenance perennial gardens. Consider using plants that perform well with little maintenance and ones that are generally pest- and disease-free.

COARSE-TEXTURED PERENNIALS

Bergenia
Black-eyed Susan
Daylily
Hollyhock
Hosta
Lungwort
Mullein
Coneflower
Rose-mallow
Sedum 'Autumn Joy'

FINE-TEXTURED PERENNIALS

Artemisia
Astilbe
Bleeding Heart
Columbine
Coreopsis
Lady's Mantle
Meadow Rue
Thyme

LOW-MAINTENANCE PERENNIALS

Ajuga*
Bergamot*
Black-eyed Susan
Coral Bells
Coreopsis
Potentilla
Daylily*
English Daisy*
Hosta
Dead Nettle*
Pinks
Pincushion Flower
Russian Sage
(*may take over garden)

Hosta (above), Bleeding Heart (below)

English Daisy (below)

GETTING STARTED

*O*nce you have some ideas about what you want in your garden, consider the growing conditions. Plants growing in ideal conditions—or conditions as close to ideal as you can get them—are healthier and less prone to pest and disease problems than plants growing in stressful conditions. Some plants considered high maintenance become low maintenance when grown in the right conditions.

Do not attempt to make your garden match the growing conditions of the plants you like. Instead, choose plants to match your garden conditions. The levels of light, the type of soil and the amount of exposure in your garden provide guidelines that make plant selection easier. A sketch of

your garden, drawn on graph paper, may help you organize the various considerations as you plan. Knowing your growing conditions can prevent costly mistakes—plan ahead rather than correct later.

LIGHT

There are four categories of light in a garden: full sun, partial shade, light shade and full shade. Available light is affected by buildings, trees, fences and the position of the sun at different times of the day and year. Knowing what light is available in your garden will help you determine where to place each plant.

Plants in full-sun locations, such as along south-facing walls, receive direct sunlight for all or most of the day. Locations classified as partial sun or partial shade, such as east- or west-facing walls, receive direct sunlight for part of the day and shade for the rest. Light-shade locations receive shade for most or all of the day, although some sunlight does filter through to ground level. An example of a light-shade location might be the ground under a small-leaved tree such as a birch. Full-shade locations, which would include the north side of a house, receive no direct sunlight. It is important to remember that the intensity of the full sun can vary. For example, heat can become trapped and magnified between buildings in a city, baking all but the most heat-tolerant of plants there in a concrete oven. Conversely, the sheltered hollow in the shade that protects your heat-hating plants in the humid summer heat may become a frost trap in the winter, killing tender plants that should otherwise survive.

Plant your perennials where they will grow best. For hot and dry areas and for low-lying, damp sections of the garden, select plants that prefer those conditions.

Sunny garden (above), shade border (below)

PERENNIALS FOR FULL SUN
Artemisia
Basket-of-gold
Coreopsis
Daylily
Mallow
Phlox
Russian Sage
Sedum
Thyme

PERENNIALS FOR FULL SHADE
Astilbe
Bleeding Heart
Dead Nettle
Hosta
Lily-of-the-valley
Lungwort
Monkshood
Primrose
Sweet Woodruff
Vinca
Violet
Wild Ginger

Artemisia for sandy soil

Primroses like acid conditions.

Sand has lots of air space and doesn't compact easily. Clay particles are the smallest and can be seen only through a microscope. Water penetrates clay very slowly and drains very slowly. Clay holds the most nutrients, but there is very little room for air, and clay compacts quite easily. Most soil is made up of a combination of different particle sizes. These soils are called loams.

PERENNIALS FOR SANDY SOIL
Artemisia
Basket-of-gold
Euphorbia
Mullein
Potentilla
Russian Sage
Thyme

PERENNIALS FOR CLAY SOIL
Ajuga
Black-eyed Susan
Foamflower
Hardy Geranium
Hosta
Lily-of-the-valley
Vinca
Yarrow

SOIL

Plants and the soil they grow in have a unique relationship. Many plant functions go on underground. Soil holds air, water, nutrients and organic matter. Plant roots depend upon these resources while using the soil to hold themselves upright.

Soil is made up of particles of different sizes. Sand particles are the largest. Water drains quickly out of sandy soil and quickly washes nutrients away.

The other aspect of soil to consider is the pH—the scale on which acidity or alkalinity is measured. Soils in Ontario vary from very acidic to very alkaline. Soil acidity influences which nutrients are available for plants. Most plants prefer a soil pH between 5.5 and 7.5. You can test your soil if you plan to amend it; testing kits are available at most garden centres. Soil can be made more alkaline with the addition of horticultural lime. Soil can be made more acidic with the addition of peat moss, pine needles or chopped oak leaves. Altering the pH of your soil takes a long time, often many years, and is not easy. If there are only one or two plants you are trying to grow that require a soil that is more or less acidic, consider growing them in a container or raised bed where it will be easier to control and amend the pH as needed.

Some perennials thrive in clay soil.

Another thing to consider is how quickly the water drains out of your soil. Rocky soil on a hillside will probably drain very quickly; plants that prefer a very well-drained soil could do well there. Low-lying areas tend to retain water longer and some areas may rarely drain at all. Moist areas can be used for plants that require a consistent water supply, and areas that stay wet can be used for plants that prefer boggy conditions. Drainage can be improved in very wet areas by adding sand or gravel to the soil or by building raised beds. Water retention in sandy soil can be improved through the addition of organic matter.

Evening Primrose (above), Lady's Mantle (below)

PERENNIALS FOR MOIST SOIL

Astilbe
Bleeding Heart
Cardinal Flower
Doronicum
Goat's Beard
Lady's Mantle
Ligularia
Lungwort
Meadowsweet
Monkshood
Primrose

Sunny, exposed garden

Beard Tongue likes exposed conditions.

PERENNIALS FOR DRY SOIL
Artemisia
Basket-of-gold
Coreopsis
Evening Primrose
Goutweed
Lamb's Ears
Lupine
Pinks
Potentilla
Russian Sage
Thrift
Yarrow

Exposure

Finally, consider the exposure in your garden. Wind, heat, cold and rain are some of the elements your garden is exposed to, and different plants are better adapted than others to withstand the potential damage of these forces. Buildings, walls, fences, hills, hedges and trees can all influence your garden's exposure.

Wind in particular can cause extensive damage to your plants. Plants can become dehydrated in windy locations because they may not be able to draw water out of the soil fast enough to replace the water that is lost through the leaves. Tall, stiff-stemmed perennials can be knocked over or broken by strong winds. Some plants that do not require staking in a sheltered location may need to be staked in a more exposed one. Use plants that are recommended for exposed locations or temper the effect of the wind with a hedge or some trees. A solid wall will create wind turbulence on the leeward side, while a looser structure, such as a hedge, breaks up the force of the wind and protects a larger area.

PERENNIALS FOR EXPOSED LOCATIONS
Basket-of-gold
Beard Tongue
Candytuft
Columbine
Creeping Phlox
Euphorbia
Goutweed
Sedum (groundcover species)
Thyme

PREPARING THE GARDEN

*T*aking the time to properly prepare your flowerbeds before you plant will save you time and effort over summer. Many gardening problems can be avoided with good preparation and maintenance. Starting out with as few weeds as possible and with well-prepared soil that has had organic material added will give your plants a good start.

Loosen the soil with a large garden fork and remove the weeds. Avoid working the soil when it is very wet or very dry because you will damage the soil structure by breaking down the pockets that hold air and water. Add organic matter and work it into the soil with a spade, fork or rototiller.

Organic matter is an important component of soil. It increases the water-holding and nutrient-holding capacity of sandy soil and binds together the large particles. In a clay soil, organic matter will increase the water-absorbing and draining potential by opening up spaces between the tiny particles. Common organic additives for your soil are grass clippings, shredded leaves, peat moss, chopped straw, well-rotted manure or composted hemlock bark.

Preparing the soil (above), weeding (below)

COMPOSTING

Any organic matter you add will be of greater benefit to your soil if it has been composted first. Adding composted organic matter to soil adds nutrients and improves soil structure.

Compost worms

Wooden compost bins (above), plastic (below)

In natural environments, such as forests or meadows, compost is created when leaves, plant bits and other debris are broken down on the soil surface. This process will also take place in your garden beds if you work fresh organic matter into the soil. However, micro-organisms that break organic matter down use the same nutrients as your plants. The tougher the organic matter, the more nutrients in the soil will be used trying to break the matter down. This will rob your plants of vital nutrients, particularly nitrogen. Also, fresh organic matter and garden debris might encourage or introduce pests and diseases in your garden.

It is best to compost organic matter before adding it to your garden beds. A compost pile or bin, which can be built or purchased, creates a controlled environment where organic matter can be fully broken down before being introduced to your garden. Good composting methods also reduce the possibility of spreading pests and diseases.

Creating compost is a simple process. Kitchen scraps, grass clippings and fall leaves will slowly break down if left in a pile. The process can be sped up by following a few simple guidelines.

Your compost pile should contain both dry and fresh materials, with a larger proportion of dry matter such as chopped straw, shredded leaves or sawdust. Fresh green matter, such as vegetable scraps, grass clippings or pulled weeds, breaks down quickly and produces nitrogen, which feeds the decomposer organisms while they break down the tougher dry matter.

Layer the green matter with the dry matter and mix in small amounts of soil from your garden or previously finished compost. The addition of soil or compost will introduce beneficial micro-organisms. If the pile seems very dry, sprinkle some water between the layers—the compost should be moist but not soaking wet, like a wrung-out sponge. Adding nitrogen, like that found in fertilizer, will speed up decomposition. Avoid strong concentrations that can kill beneficial organisms.

Each week or two, use a pitchfork to turn the pile over or poke holes into it. This will help aerate the material, which will speed up decomposition. A compost pile that is kept aerated can generate a lot of heat. Temperatures can reach up to 71° C (160° F). Such a high temperature will destroy weed seeds and kill many damaging organisms. Most beneficial organisms will not be killed unless the temperature rises higher than this. To monitor the temperature of the compost near the middle of the pile you will need a thermometer that is attached to a long probe, similar to a large meat thermometer. Turn your compost once the temperature drops. Turning and aerating the pile will stimulate the process to heat up again. The pile can be left to sit without turning and will eventually be ready to use if you are willing to wait several months to a year.

Materials (above), compost thermometer (below)

When you can no longer recognize the matter you put into the compost bin and the temperature no longer rises upon turning, your compost is ready to be mixed into your garden beds. Getting to this point can take as little as one month and will leave you with organic material rich in nutrients and beneficial organisms.

Compost can also be purchased from most garden centres. Whether you use your own or store-bought compost, mix a layer into a bed when you prepare it or add a trowelful of compost to the planting hole and mix it into the garden soil when adding perennials to an established bed.

SELECTING PERENNIALS

*P*erennials can be purchased as plants or seeds. Purchased plants may begin flowering the same year they are planted, while plants started from seed may take several years to mature. Starting plants from seed is more economical. (Read about starting perennials from seed in the Propagation section, p. 42.)

Plants and seeds are available from many sources. Garden centres, mail-order catalogues and friends and neighbours are excellent sources of perennials. Garden societies, public gardens and gardening clubs may also exchange or sell seeds and plants. Get your perennials from a reputable source, and be sure that the plants are not diseased or pest-ridden.

Purchased plants come in two main forms: either in pots or bare-root, usually packed in moist peat moss or sawdust. Potted perennials are growing and have probably been raised in the pot. Bare-root perennials are typically dormant, although some of the previous year's growth may be evident or there may be new growth starting. Both potted and bare-root perennials are good purchases, and in each case there are things to look for to make sure that you are getting a plant of the best quality.

Potted plants come in many sizes. Though a larger plant may appear more mature, it may be better to choose a smaller one that will suffer less from the shock of being transplanted. Most perennials grow quickly

Plant on right is not rootbound, thus healthier.

Rootbound plant

once they are planted. Select plants that seem to be a good size for the pot they are in. When tapped lightly out of the pot, the roots should be visible but not winding and twisting around the inside of the pot. The leaves should be a healthy colour.

If the leaves appear to be chewed or damaged, check carefully for insects or diseases before you purchase the plant. If the plants are diseased, do not purchase them. If you find insects on the plant, you may not want to purchase it

unless you are willing to cope with the hitchhikers you are taking home. To avoid spreading the pest, deal with any pest problems before you move the plants into the garden.

Once you get your plants home, water them if they are dry and keep them in a lightly shaded location until you plant them. Remove any damaged growth and discard it. Plant your new perennials into the garden as soon as possible.

Bare-root plants are most commonly sold through mail order, but some are available in garden centres, usually in the spring. Choose roots that are dormant (without top growth). If a bare-root plant has been trying to grow in the stressful conditions of a plastic bag, it may have too little energy to recover and may take longer to establish itself in the garden once planted.

Cut off any damaged parts of the roots with a very sharp knife. Bare-root perennials will dehydrate quickly out of soil, so they need to be planted more quickly than potted plants. Soak the roots in lukewarm water and plant them either directly in the garden or into pots with good quality potting soil until they can be moved to the garden.

It can be difficult to distinguish the top from the bottom of some bare-root plants. Usually there is a tell-tale dip or stub at the top from which the plant previously grew. If you can't find any distinguishing characteristics, lay the root in the ground on its side and the plant will send the roots down and the shoots up.

PLANTING PERENNIALS

Once you have your garden planned, the soil well prepared and the perennials ready, it is time to plant. If your perennials have identification tags, be sure to poke them into the soil next to the newly planted perennials. Next spring, when most of your perennial bed is nothing but a few stubs of green, the tags will help you with identification and remind you that there is indeed a plant in that bare patch of soil.

POTTED PERENNIALS

Perennials in pots are convenient because you can space them out across the bed or rearrange them before you start to dig. To prevent the roots from drying out, do not unpot the plant until immediately before

you transplant. Once you have the collection organized, you can begin planting.

To plant potted perennials, start by digging a hole about the width and depth of the pot. Remove the perennial from the pot. If the pot is small enough, you can hold your hand across the top of the pot, letting your fingers straddle the stem of the plant, and then turn it upside down. Never pull on the stem or leaves to get a plant out of a pot. It is better to cut a difficult pot off rather than risk damaging the plant. Tease a few roots out of the soil ball to get the plant growing in the right direction. If the roots have become densely wound around the inside of the pot, you should cut into the root mass with a sharp knife

Support the plant as you pull off the pot; gently remove the pot.

to encourage new growth into the surrounding soil. The process of cutting into the bottom half of the root ball and spreading the two halves of the mass outward like butterfly wings is called 'butterflying the roots' and is a very effective way to promote fast growth of pot-bound perennials that are being transplanted. Place the plant into the prepared hole. It should be buried to the same level that it was at in the pot, or a little higher, to allow for the soil to settle. If the plant is too low in the ground, it may rot when rain collects around the crown. Fill the soil in around the roots and firm it down. Water the plant well as soon as you have planted it and regularly until it has established itself.

BARE-ROOT PERENNIALS

During planting, bare-root perennials should not be spaced out across the bed unless they are already in pots. Roots dry out very quickly if you leave them lying about waiting to be planted. If you want to visualize your spacing, you can poke sticks into the ground or put rocks down to represent the perennials.

If you have been keeping your bare-root perennials in potting soil, you may find that the roots have not grown enough to knit the soil together and that all the soil falls away from the root when you remove it from the pot. Don't be concerned. Simply follow the regular root-planting instructions. If the soil does hold together, plant the root the way you would a potted perennial.

ROOT TYPES

The type of hole you need to dig will depend on the type of roots the perennial has. Plants with **fibrous roots** will need a mound of soil in the centre of the planting hole over which the roots can be spread out evenly.

Loosen the root ball before firming it into the ground.

The hole should be dug as deep as the longest roots. Mound the soil into the centre of the hole up to ground level. Spread the roots out around the mound and cover them with loosened soil. If you are adding just one or two plants and do not want to prepare an entire bed, dig a hole twice as wide and deep as the root ball and amend the soil with composted manure mixed with peat moss. Add a slow-release organic fertilizer to the back-fill of soil that you spread around the plant. Fresh chicken or barnyard manure can also be used to improve small areas, but it should be placed in the bottom of the planting hole. Add a layer of soil on top of the manure before you add the plant. Roots that come in contact with fresh manure will suffer fertilizer burn.

Plants with a **tap root** need to be planted in a hole that is narrow and about as deep as the root is long. Use a trowel to open up a suitable hole, tuck the root into it and fill it in again with the soil around it. If you can't tell which end is up, plant the root on its side.

Some plants have roots that appear to be tap roots, but the plant seems to be growing off the side of the root rather than upwards from one end. These roots are called **rhizomes**. Iris roots are rhizomes. Rhizomes should be planted horizontally in a shallow hole and covered with soil.

In most cases, you should try to get the crown at or just above soil level and loosen the surrounding soil in the planting hole. Keep the roots thoroughly watered until the plants are well established.

Whether the plants are potted or bare-root, it is good to leave them alone and let them recover from the

Sedum, Catmint and annuals in a planter

gardens with very poor soil or in yards where kids and dogs might destroy a traditional perennial bed. Many perennials such as hostas and daylilies can grow in the same container without any fresh potting soil for five or six years. Be sure to fertilize and water perennials in planters more often than those growing in the ground. Dig your finger deep into the soil around the perennial to see if it needs water. Too much water in the planter causes root rot.

Always use a good quality potting mix or a soil mix intended for containers in your planters. Garden soil quickly loses its structure when used in a container and becomes a solid lump, preventing air, water and roots from penetrating into the soil. Plants will never thrive in a container if planted in soil from the garden. At the very least mix half garden soil with half peat moss and mix the two together well.

When designing a planter garden, you can either keep one type of perennial in each planter and display many planters together or mix different perennials in large planters along with annuals and bulbs. The latter choice results in a dynamic bouquet of flowers and foliage. Keep the tall upright perennials such as yarrow in the centre of the planter, the rounded or bushy types such as coreopsis around the sides and low-growing or draping perennials such as candytuft along the edge of the planter. Perennials that have long bloom times or attractive foliage are good for planters.

stress of planting. In the first month, you will need only to water the plant regularly, weed around it and watch for pests. A mulch spread on the bed around your plants will keep in moisture and control weeds.

If you have prepared your beds properly, you probably won't have to fertilize in the first year. If you do want to fertilize, wait until your new plants have started healthy new growth and apply only a weak fertilizer to avoid damaging the new root growth.

PLANTERS

Perennials can also be grown in planters for portable displays that can be moved about the garden. Planters can also be used on patios or decks, in

Choose hardy perennials that can tolerate difficult conditions. Planters are exposed to extremes of our variable weather—baking hot in summer and freezing cold in winter. Perennials in planters dry out quickly in hot weather and become waterlogged after a couple of rainy days. Not all perennials are tough enough to survive in these extreme conditions. Some of the more invasive perennials are a good choice for planters because their spread is controlled but at the same time they are very tough to kill.

Because the exposed sides of a container provide little insulation for roots and containers allow for greater fluctuations in temperature, perennials in planters are more susceptible to winter damage. The container itself may even crack when exposed to a deep freeze. Don't despair—there are plenty of things you can do to get planters through a tough Ontario winter in great shape. The simplest thing you can do is move the planter to a sheltered spot. Most perennials do require some cold in winter in order to flower the next year, so find a spot that is still cold but provides some shelter. An unheated garage or an enclosed porch is a good place; even your garden shed will offer your plants more protection than they would get sitting in the great outdoors, exposed to the elements.

If you haven't got the space or access to these places, consider your basement window wells. These are sheltered, below ground and have a nearby source of some heat from the window. Wait until your pots have

Mixed perennials in a planter

frozen. Layer straw at the bottom of the well, set your pots on the straw, then cover them with more straw. Waiting until the pots freeze prevents rot and can also help deter the biggest problem: mice. Mice find the straw is a comfortable home and the perennial roots a tasty treat, but they are less likely to dig into frozen soil to get to the roots. If mice do present a problem, consider sprinkling some commercial mouse bait around the pots. If you don't want to use poisons, place a layer of styrofoam insulation under and on top of the pots; the styrofoam will protect the pots without being quite so appealing to small rodents.

The pots themselves can be winterproofed before you plant your perennials. Layer styrofoam insulation or 'packing peanuts' at the bottom of the pot and around the inside of the planter before you add your soil and plants. Make sure excess water can still drain freely from the container. Commercial planter-insulating materials are available at garden centres. Insulating pots is particularly useful for high-rise dwellers with balcony gardens. This insulation will also protect the roots from excessive heat in the summer.

Finally, planters can be buried in the garden for the winter. Find an open space in a flower bed and dig a hole deep enough to allow you to sink the planter up to its rim. This can be messy, particularly in the spring when

you dig the planter up. This method also requires enough empty space in the garden to fit your planter or planters. Large planters may require an extensive excavation or even the use of a backhoe in order to dig deeply enough to fit the entire pot.

PERENNIALS FOR PLANTERS
Beard Tongue
Candytuft
Catmint
Daylily
Dead Nettle
Goat's Beard
Goutweed
Hardy Geranium
Hosta
Lady's Mantle
Pincushion Flower
Pinks
Potentilla
Sedum
Snow-in-Summer
Tansy
Speedwell
Yarrow

Mixed display of perennials and annuals in an old wheelbarrow

CARING FOR PERENNIALS

*M*any perennials require little care, but all will benefit from a few maintenance basics. Weeding, watering and grooming are just a few of the chores that, when done on a regular basis, keep major work to a minimum.

WEEDING

Controlling weeds is one of the most important things you will have to do in your garden. Besides being unsightly, weeds compete with your perennials for light, nutrients and space. Weeds can also harbour pests and diseases. Try to prevent weeds from germinating. If they do germinate, pull them out while they are still small and before they have a chance to flower, set seed and start a whole new generation of problems.

Weeds can be pulled out by hand or with a hoe. Quickly scuffing across the soil surface with the hoe will pull out small weeds and sever larger ones from their roots. A layer of mulch is an excellent way to suppress weeds.

MULCHING

Mulches are an important gardening tool. They prevent weed seeds from germinating by blocking out the light. Soil temperatures remain more consistent and more moisture is retained under a layer of mulch. Mulch also prevents soil erosion during heavy rain or strong winds. Organic mulches can consist of compost, bark chips, shredded leaves or grass clippings. Organic mulches are desirable because they improve the soil and add nutrients as they break down.

The soil in this garden is protected by mulch.

In spring, spread about 5–10 cm (2–4") of mulch over your perennial beds around your plants. Keep the area immediately around the crown or stem of your plants clear. Mulch that is too close to your plants can trap moisture and prevent good air circulation, encouraging disease. If the layer of mulch disappears into the soil over summer, you should replenish it.

A fresh layer of mulch, up to 10 cm (4") thick, can be laid once the ground freezes in fall to protect the plants over winter. This is particularly important if you can't depend on a steady layer of snow to cover your garden in the winter, as is the case in much of southern Ontario. You can cover the plants with dry material such as chopped straw, pine needles or shredded leaves. Keep in mind that as the ground freezes, so too may your pile of potential mulch. One solution is to cover most of the bed with mulch, leaving only the plants exposed, before the ground freezes. Put extra mulch, enough to cover the plants, in a large plastic bag or your wheelbarrow and put it somewhere that will take longer to freeze, perhaps in your garage or the garden shed. Once the ground is completely frozen, you will have a supply of unfrozen mulch that you can use to cover the plants.

In late winter or early spring, once the weather starts to warm up, pull the mulch layer off the plants and see if they have started growing. If they have, you can pull the mulch back, but keep it nearby in case you need to put it back on to protect the tender new growth from a late frost. Once your plants are well on their way and you are no longer worried about frost, you can remove the protective mulch completely. Compost the old mulch and apply a new spring and summer mulch.

WATERING

Watering is another basic of perennial care. Many perennials need little supplemental watering if they have been planted in their preferred conditions and are given a moisture-retaining mulch. The rule of watering is to water thoroughly and infrequently. When you do water, make sure the water penetrates at least 10 cm (4") into the soil. Consult your local garden centre for information on irrigation systems.

FERTILIZING

If you prepare your beds well and add new compost to them each spring, you should not need to add extra fertilizer. If you have a limited amount of compost, you can mix a slow-release fertilizer into the soil around your perennials in the spring. Some plants, e.g., delphinium, are heavy feeders that need additional supplements throughout the growing season.

There are many organic and chemical fertilizers available at garden centres. Be sure to use the recommended quantity because too much fertilizer will do more harm than good. Roots can be burned by fertilizer that is applied in high concentrations. Problems are more likely to be caused by chemical fertilizers because they are more concentrated than organic fertilizers.

GROOMING

Many perennials will benefit from a bit of grooming. Resilient plants, plentiful blooming and compact growth are the signs of a well-groomed garden. Thinning, pinching, disbudding, staking and deadheading plants will enhance the beauty of a perennial garden. The methods are simple, but you will have to experiment in order to get the right effect in your own garden.

Thinning is done to clump-forming perennials such as black-eyed Susan, coneflower or bergamot early in the season when shoots have just emerged. These plants develop a dense clump of stems that allows very little air or light into the centre of the plant. Remove half the shoots when they first emerge to increase air circulation and prevent diseases such as powdery mildew. The increased light encourages more compact growth and more flowers. Throughout the growing season, thin any growth that is weak, diseased or growing in the wrong direction.

Trimming or **pinching** perennials is a simple procedure, but timing it correctly and achieving just the right look can be tricky. Early in the year, before the flower buds have appeared, trim the plant to encourage new side shoots. Remove the tip and some stems of the plant just above a leaf or pair of leaves. This can be done stem by stem, but if you have a lot of plants you can trim off the tops with your hedge shears to one-third of the height you expect the plants to reach. The growth that begins to emerge can

Coneflower

Black-eyed Susan

Give plants enough time to set buds and flower. Continual pinching will encourage very dense growth but also delay flowering. Most spring-flowering plants cannot be pinched back or they will not flower. Early summer or mid-summer bloomers should be pinched only once, as early in the season as possible. Late summer and fall bloomers can be pinched several times but should be left alone past June. Don't pinch the plant if flower buds have formed—it may not have enough energy or time left in the year to develop a new set of buds. Experimenting and keeping detailed notes will improve your pinching skills.

Disbudding is another grooming stage. This is the removal of some flower buds to encourage the remaining ones to produce larger flowers. This technique is popular with peony growers.

Staking, the use of poles or wires to hold plants erect, can often be avoided by astute thinning and pinching, but there are always a few plants that will need a bit of support to look their best in your garden. There are three basic types of stakes used for the different growth habits that need support. Plants that develop tall spikes such as hollyhock, delphinium and sometimes foxglove require each spike to be staked individually. A strong narrow pole such as a bamboo stick can be pushed into the ground early in the year and the spike tied to the stake as it grows. A forked branch can also be used to support single-stem plants.

be pinched again. Beautiful layered effects can be achieved by staggering the trimming times by a week or two.

PERENNIALS TO TRIM EARLY IN THE SEASON
Artemisia
Bergamot
Black-eyed Susan
Catmint
Coneflower
Mallow
Sedum 'Autumn Joy'
Shasta Daisy

Many plants, such as peonies, get a bit top heavy as they grow and tend to flop over once they reach a certain height. A wire hoop, sometimes called a peony ring, is the most unobtrusive way to hold up such a plant. When the plant is young, the legs of the peony ring are pushed into the ground around it, and as the plant grows, it is supported by the wire ring. At the same time, the bushy growth hides the ring. Wire tomato cages can also be used to support peonies.

Other plants, such as coreopsis, form a floppy tangle of stems. These plants can be given a bit of support with twiggy branches inserted into the ground around the young plants; the plants then grow up into the twigs.

Spiral stakes (above), wire support hoops (below)

Some people consider stakes to be unsightly no matter how hidden they seem to be. There are a few things you can do to reduce the need for staking. First, grow the plant in the right conditions. Don't assume a plant will do better in a richer soil than is recommended. Very rich soil causes many plants to produce weak, leggy growth that is prone to falling over. Also, a plant that likes full sun will be stretched out and leggy if grown in shade. Second, use other plants for support. Mix in plants that have a more stable structure between plants that need support. A plant may still fall over slightly, but only as far as its neighbour will allow. Finally, look for compact varieties that don't require staking.

Astilbe in need of support (below)

Deadheading Asters (above), Astilbe (below)

Drying Poppy seedheads (below)

Deadheading, the removal of flowers once they are finished blooming, serves several purposes. It keeps plants looking tidy, prevents the plant from spreading seeds (and therefore seedlings) throughout the garden, often prolongs blooming and helps prevent pest and disease problems.

Deadheading is not necessary for every plant. Seedheads of some plants are left in place to provide interest in the garden over winter. Other plants are short-lived, and leaving some of the seedheads in place encourages future generations to replace the old plants. Hollyhock is one example of a short-lived perennial that re-seeds. In some cases the self-sown seedlings do not possess the attractive features of the parent plant. Deadheading may be required in these cases.

PERENNIALS WITH INTERESTING SEEDHEADS
Astilbe
Coneflower
False Solomon's Seal
Goat's Beard
Meadowsweet
Oriental Poppy
Pasque Flower
Russian Sage
Sedum 'Autumn Joy'
Tansy

PERENNIALS THAT SELF-SEED

Ajuga (variable seedlings)
Bleeding Heart (variable seedlings)
Cardinal Flower
Corydalis
Foxglove
Hollyhock (variable seedlings)
Lady's Mantle
Lupine
Mallow
Mullein
Pinks
Maltese Cross
Violet

Both Ajuga and Lady's Mantle self-seed.

Flowers can be deadheaded by hand or snipped off with hand pruners. Bushy plants that have many tiny flowers, particularly ones that have a short bloom period such as basket-of-gold, can be more aggressively pruned back with garden shears once they are done flowering. For some plants—such as creeping phlox—shearing will promote new growth and possibly encourage blooms later in the season.

Shear False Rockcress (above), Creeping Phlox (below).

PERENNIALS TO SHEAR BACK AFTER BLOOMING

Basket-of-gold
Candytuft
Creeping Phlox
Bellflower
Goutweed
Hardy Geranium
Marguerite Daisy
Dead Nettle
False Rockcress
Snow-in-summer
Sweet Woodruff
Thyme
Yarrow

PROPAGATION

*L*earning to propagate your own perennials is an interesting and challenging aspect of gardening that can save you money but also requires time and space. Seeds, cuttings and divisions are the three methods of increasing your perennial population. There are benefits and problems associated with each method.

SEEDS

Starting perennials from seed is a great way to propagate a large number of plants at a relatively low cost. Seeds can be purchased or collected from your own or a friend's perennial garden. There are some limitations to propagating from seed. Some cultivars and varieties don't pass on their desirable traits to their offspring.

Other perennials have seeds that take a very long time to germinate, if they germinate at all, and may take an even longer time to grow to flowering size. However, many perennials grow easily from seed and flower within a year or two of being transplanted into the garden. There are challenges and limitations to starting perennials from seed, but the work will be worth it when you see the plants you raised from tiny seedlings finally begin to flower.

Specific propagation information is given for each plant, but there are a few basic rules for starting all seeds. Some seeds can be started directly in the garden, but it is easier to control temperature and moisture levels and to provide a sterile environment if you start the seeds indoors. Seeds can be started in pots or, if you need a lot of plants, flats. Use a sterile soil mix intended for starting seeds. The soil will generally need to be kept moist but not soggy. Most seeds germinate in moderately warm temperatures of about 14°–21° C (57°–70° F).

There are many seed-starting supplies available at garden centres. Some supplies are useful but many are not necessary. Seed-tray dividers are useful. These dividers, often called plug trays, are made of plastic and prevent the roots from tangling with the roots of the other plants and from being disturbed when seedlings are transplanted. Heating coils or pads can be useful. Placed under the pots or flats, they keep the soil at a constant temperature.

All seedlings are susceptible to a problem called 'damping off,' which is caused by soil-borne fungi. An afflicted seedling looks as though someone has pinched the stem at soil

level, causing the plant to topple over. The pinched area blackens and the seedling dies. Sterile soil mix, good air circulation and evenly moist soil will help prevent this problem.

Fill your pot or seed tray with the soil mix and firm it down slightly—not too firmly or the soil will not drain. Wet the soil before planting your seeds. Seeds may wash into clumps if the soil is watered after the seeds are planted. Large seeds can be placed individually and spaced out in pots or trays. If you have divided inserts for your trays, you can plant one or two seeds per section. Small seeds may have to be sprinkled in a bit more randomly. Fold a sheet of paper in half and place the small seeds in the crease. Gently tapping the underside of the fold will bounce or roll the seeds off the paper in a more controlled manner. Some seeds are so tiny that they look like dust. These seeds can be mixed with a small quantity of very fine sand and spread on the soil surface. These tiny seeds may not need to

Preparing seed tray

Using folded paper to plant small seeds

Spray bottle provides a gentle mist for seeds.

Start Lupines (above), Pinks (below) from seed.

Foxglove (below) self-seeds readily.

be covered with any more soil. The medium-sized seeds can be lightly covered and the larger seeds can be pressed into the soil and then lightly covered. Do not cover seeds that need to be exposed to light in order to germinate. Water the seeds using a very fine spray if the soil starts to dry out. A hand-held spray bottle will moisten the soil without disturbing the seeds.

Plant only one type of seed in each pot or flat. Each species has a different rate of germination, and the germinated seedlings will require different conditions than the seeds that have yet to germinate. To keep the environment moist, you can place pots inside clear plastic bags. Change the bag or turn it inside out once the condensation starts to build up and drip. Plastic bags can be held up with stakes or wires poked in around the edges of the pot. Many seed trays come with clear plastic covers which can be placed over the flats to keep the moisture in. Plastic can be removed once the seeds have germinated.

Seeds generally do not require a lot of light in order to germinate, so pots or trays can be kept in a warm, out of the way place. Once the seeds have germinated, they can be placed in a bright location but out of direct sun. Plants should be transplanted to individual pots once they have three or four true leaves. True leaves are the ones that look like the mature leaves. (The first one or two leaves are actually part of the seed.) Plants in plug trays can be left until neighbouring leaves start to touch each other. At this point the plants will be competing for light and should be transplanted to individual pots.

Young seedlings do not need to be fertilized. Fertilizer will cause seedlings to produce soft, spindly growth that is susceptible to attack by insects and diseases. The seed itself provides all the nutrition the seedling will need. A fertilizer, diluted to one-quarter or one-half strength, can be used once seedlings have four or five true leaves.

Seed scratching (scarification) with sandpaper
Below, preparing seeds for cold treatment

Seeds have protective devices that prevent them from germinating when conditions are not favourable or from all germinating at once. In the wild, staggered germination periods improve the chances of survival. Many seeds will easily grow as soon as they are planted, but others need to have their defences lowered before they will germinate. Some seeds also produce poisonous chemicals in the seed coats to deter insects.

PERENNIALS TO START FROM SEED
Corydalis
Delphinium
Pinks
Foxglove
Hollyhock
Lady's Mantle
Lupine
Maltese Cross

You can force seeds to sprout by mimicking natural conditions. Some thick-coated seeds can be soaked for a day or two in a glass of water to promote germination. This mimics the end of the dry season and the beginning of the rainy season, which is when the plant would germinate in its natural environment. The water softens the seed coat and in some cases washes away the chemicals that have been preventing germination. Rose-mallow is an example of a plant with seeds that need to be soaked before germinating.

Other thick-coated seeds need to have their seed coats scratched to allow moisture to penetrate the seed coat and prompt germination. In nature, birds scratch the seeds with gravel in their craws and acid in their stomachs. Nick the seeds with a knife or gently rub them between two sheets of sand paper. Leave the seeds in a dry place for a day or so after scratching them before planting to give the seeds a chance to get ready for germination before they are exposed to water. Lupines and anemones have seeds that need their thick coats scratched.

Shade cloth protecting plants in cold frame

Plastic dome protecting a patio bed

Plants from northern climates often have seeds that wait until spring before they germinate. These seeds must be exposed to a period of cold, which mimics winter, before they will germinate. One method of cold treatment is to plant the seeds in a pot or tray and place them in the refrigerator for up to two months. Check the container regularly and don't allow these to dry out. This method is fairly simple but not very practical if your refrigerator is as crowded as mine. Yarrow, bergenia and primrose have seeds that respond to cold treatment.

A less space-consuming method is to mix the seeds with some moistened sand, peat or sphagnum moss. Place the mix in a sealable sandwich bag and pop it in the refrigerator for up to two months, again being sure the sand or moss doesn't dry out. The seeds can then be planted in the pot or tray. Spread the seeds and the moist sand or moss onto the prepared surface and press it all down gently.

A cold frame is a wonderful tool for the gardener. It can be used to protect tender plants over the winter, to start vegetable seeds early in spring, to harden plants off before moving them to the garden, to protect fall-germinating seedlings and young cuttings or divisions and to start seeds that need a cold treatment. This mini-greenhouse structure is built so that ground level on the inside of the cold frame is lower than on the outside. The angled, hinged lid is fitted with glass. The soil around the outside of the cold frame insulates the plants inside. The lid lets light in and collects some heat during the day and prevents rain from damaging tender plants. If the interior gets too hot, the lid can be raised for ventilation. A hot frame is insulated and has heating coils in the floor to prevent the soil from freezing or to maintain a constant soil temperature for germinating seeds or rooting cuttings.

CUTTINGS

Cuttings are an excellent way to propagate varieties and cultivars that you really like but that don't come true from seed or don't produce seed at all. Each cutting will grow into a reproduction (clone) of the parent plant. Cuttings are taken from the stems of some perennials and the roots of others.

Stem cuttings are generally taken in spring and early summer. During this time plants go through a flush of fresh, new growth, either before or after flowering. Avoid taking cuttings from plants that are in flower. Plants that are in flower, or are about to flower, are busy trying to reproduce; plants that are busy growing, by contrast, are already full of the right hormones to promote quick root growth. If you do take cuttings from plants that are flowering, be sure to remove the flowers and the buds to divert the plant's energy back into growing.

Large numbers of cuttings don't often result in as many plants. To root, cuttings need to be kept in a warm humid place, which makes them prone to fungal diseases. Providing proper sanitation and encouraging quick rooting will increase the survival rate of your cuttings.

Propagate Catmint (above) from stem cuttings.

PERENNIALS TO PROPAGATE FROM STEM CUTTINGS
Artemisia
Aster
Basket-of-gold
Beard Tongue
Bellflower
Bleeding Heart
Candytuft
Catmint
Coreopsis
Euphorbia
False Rockcress
Mullein
Pinks
Potentilla
Sedum 'Autumn Joy'
Snow-in-summer
Thyme
Speedwell
Violet
Yarrow

There is no absolute measurement for what size cuttings should be. Some gardeners believe that smaller cuttings are more likely to root and will root more quickly. Other gardeners claim that larger cuttings

Removing lower leaves

Dipping in rooting hormone

develop more roots and become established more quickly once planted in the garden. You may wish to try different sizes to see what works best for you. Generally, a small cutting is 2–5 cm (1–2") long and a large cutting is 10–15 cm (4–6") long.

Another way to determine the size of cuttings is to count the number of leaf nodes on the cutting. You will want at least three or four nodes on a cutting. The node is where the leaf joins the stem and where the new roots will grow from. The base of the cutting will be just below a node. Strip the leaves gently from the first and second nodes and plant the cutting below the soil. The new plants will grow from the nodes above the soil. The leaves can be left in place on the cutting above ground. If there is a lot of space between nodes, your cutting will need to be longer than the guidelines mentioned above. Some plants have almost no space at all between nodes. Cut these plants to the recommended length and gently remove the leaves from the lower half of the cutting. Plants with several nodes close together often root quickly and abundantly.

Firming the cutting into soil

Always use a sharp, sterile knife to make the cuttings. Cuts should be made straight across the stem. Once you have stripped the leaves, you can dip the end of the cutting into a rooting-hormone powder intended for softwood cuttings. Sprinkle the powder onto a piece of paper and dip the cuttings into it. Discard any extra powder left on the paper to prevent the spread of disease. Tap or blow the extra powder off the cutting. Cuttings caked with rooting hormone are more likely to rot rather than root and they do not root any faster than those that are lightly dusted. Your cuttings are now prepared for planting.

The sooner you plant your cuttings the better. The less water the cuttings

New top growth

Healthy roots

lose, the less likely they are to wilt and the more quickly they will root. Cuttings can be planted in a similar manner to seeds. Use sterile soil mix, intended for seeds or cuttings, in pots or trays that can be covered with plastic to keep in the humidity. Other mixes to root the cuttings in are sterilized sand, perlite, vermiculite or a combination of the three. Firm the soil down and moisten it before you start planting. Poke a hole in the surface of the soil with a pencil or similar object, tuck the cutting in and gently firm the soil around it. Make sure the lowest leaves do not touch the soil and that the cuttings are spaced far enough apart that adjoining leaves do not touch each other. Pots can be placed inside plastic bags. Push stakes or wires into the soil around the edge of the pot so that the plastic will be held off the leaves. The rigid plastic lids that are available for trays may not be high enough to fit over the cuttings, in which case you will have to use stakes and a plastic bag to cover the tray.

Keep the cuttings in a warm place, about 18–21° C (65–70° F), in bright indirect light. A couple of holes poked

in the bag will create some ventilation. Turn the bag inside out when condensation becomes heavy. Keep the soil moist. A hand-held mister will gently moisten the soil without disturbing the cuttings.

Most cuttings will require from one to four weeks to root. After two weeks, give the cutting a gentle tug. You will feel resistance if roots have formed. If the cutting feels as though it can pull out of the soil, then gently push it back down and leave it for longer. New growth is also a good sign that your cutting has rooted. Some gardeners simply leave the cuttings alone until they can see roots through the holes in the bottoms of the pots. Uncover the cuttings once they have developed roots.

Apply a foliar feed when the cuttings are showing new leaf growth. Plants quickly absorb nutrients through the leaves; by using a foliar feed, you can avoid stressing the newly formed roots. Your local garden centre should have foliar feeds and information about applying them. You can use your hand-held mister to apply foliar feeds.

Start Euphorbia from basal cuttings.

bases. Often, the plantlets will already have a few roots growing. The young plants develop quickly and may even grow to flowering size the first summer. You may have to cut back some of the top growth of the shoot because the tiny developing roots won't be able to support a lot of top growth. Treat these cuttings in the same way you would a stem cutting. Use a sterile knife to cut out the shoot. Sterile soil mix and humid conditions are preferred. Pot plants individually or place them in soft soil in the garden until new growth appears and roots have developed.

Once your cuttings are rooted and have had a bit of a chance to establish themselves, they can be potted individually. If you rooted several cuttings in one pot or tray, you may find that the roots have tangled together. If gentle pulling doesn't separate them, take the entire clump that is tangled together and try rinsing some of the soil away. This should free the roots enough for you to separate the plants.

Pot the young plants in a sterile potting soil. They can be moved into a sheltered area of the garden or a cold frame and grown in pots until they are large enough to plant in the garden. The plants may need some protection over the first winter. Keep them in the cold frame if they are still in pots. Give them an extra layer of mulch if they have been planted out.

Basal cuttings involve removing the new growth from the main clump and rooting it in the same manner as stem cuttings. Many plants send up new shoots or plantlets around their

PERENNIALS TO START FROM BASAL CUTTINGS

Ajuga
Bellflower
Bergamot
Catmint
Daylily
Dead Nettle
Delphinium
Euphorbia
Hardy Geranium
Hens and Chicks
Hollyhock
Lupine
Phlox
Pincushion Flower
Sedum

Root cuttings can also be taken from some plants. Dandelions are often inadvertently propagated this way: even the smallest piece of root left in the ground can sprout a new plant, foiling every attempt to eradicate them from lawns and flower beds. But there are perennials that have this ability as well. The main difference between starting root cuttings and stem cuttings is that the root cuttings must be kept fairly dry because they can rot very easily.

Cuttings can be taken from the fleshy roots of certain perennials that do not propagate well from stem cuttings. These cuttings should be taken in early or mid-spring when the ground is just starting to warm up and the roots are just about to break dormancy. At this time, the roots of the perennials are full of nutrients, which the plants stored the previous summer and fall, and hormones are initiating growth. You may have to wet the soil around the plant so that you can loosen it enough to get to the roots.

Propagate Sedum from root cuttings.

Keep the roots slightly moist, but not wet, while you are rooting them, and keep track of which end is up. Roots must be planted in a vertical, not horizontal, position in the soil, and roots need to be kept in the orientation they held while previously attached to the parent plant. There are different tricks people use to differentiate the top from the bottom of the roots. One method is to cut straight across the tops and diagonally across the bottoms.

You do not want very young or very old roots. Very young roots are usually white and quite soft; very old roots are tough and woody. The roots you should use will be tan in colour and still fleshy. To prepare your root, cut out the section you will be using with a sterile knife. Cut the root into pieces that are 2.5–5 cm (1–2") long. Remove any side roots before planting

the sections in pots or planting trays. You can use the same type of soil mix in the pots as you would for planting seeds and stem cuttings. Poke the pieces vertically into the soil and leave a tiny bit of the end poking up out of the soil. Remember to keep the pieces the right way up.

Keep the pots or trays in a warm place out of direct sunlight. Avoid overwatering them. They will send up new shoots once they have rooted and can be planted in the same manner as the stem cuttings (see p. 49).

PERENNIALS TO PROPAGATE FROM ROOT CUTTINGS
Black-eyed Susan
Bleeding Heart
Evening Primrose
Japanese Anemone
Mullein
Oriental Poppy
Phlox
Primrose
Sedum

Increase your Hardy Geraniums and Irises by rhizomes.

Dig up a section of rhizome. If you look closely at it you will see that it appears to be growing in sections. The places where these sections join are called nodes. It is from these nodes that feeder roots (smaller stringy roots) extend downwards and new plants sprout upwards. You may even see that small plants are already sprouting. The rhizome should be cut into pieces. Each piece should have at least one of these nodes in it.

Fill a pot or planting tray to about 2.5 cm (1") from the top of the container with perlite, vermiculite or seeding soil. Moisten the soil and let the excess water drain away. Lay the rhizome pieces flat on the top of the mix and almost cover them with more of the soil mix. Leaving a small bit of the top exposed to the light will encourage the shoots to sprout. The soil does not have to be kept consistently wet; to avoid rot, let your rhizome dry out between waterings. Once your cuttings have established themselves, they can be potted individually and grown in the same manner as stem cuttings (see p. 49).

PERENNIALS TO PROPAGATE FROM RHIZOMES
Bellflower
Bergenia
Hardy Geranium
Iris
Lily-of-the-valley
Wild Ginger

Rhizomes are the easiest root-type cuttings with which to propagate plants. Rhizomes are thick, fleshy root-like stems that grow horizontally along the ground, or just under the soil. Periodically, they send up new shoots from along the length of the rhizome. In this way the plant spreads. It is easy to take advantage of this feature. Take rhizome cuttings when the plant is growing vigorously, usually in late spring or early summer.

DIVISIONS

Division is quite possibly the easiest way to propagate perennials. As most perennials grow, they form larger and larger clumps. Dividing this clump once it gets big will rejuvenate the plant, keep its size in check and provide you with more plants. If a plant you really want is expensive, consider buying only one because within a few years you may have more than you can handle.

Digging up perennials for division

How often a perennial needs dividing or can be divided will vary. Some perennials, such as astilbe, need dividing almost every year to keep them vigorous, while others, such as peonies, should never be divided or need special care when they are divided. Each perennial entry in the book gives recommendations for division. In general, watch for several signs that a perennial should be divided:
• the centre of the plant has died out
• the plant is no longer flowering as profusely as it did in previous years
• the plant is encroaching on the growing space of other plants sharing the bed.

Clump of stems, roots and crowns

It is relatively easy to divide perennials. Begin by digging up the entire clump and knocking any large clods of soil away from the root ball. The clump can then be split into several pieces. A small plant with fibrous roots can be torn into sections by hand. A large plant can be pried apart with a pair of garden forks inserted back to back into the clump. Plants with thicker tuberous or rhizomatous roots can be cut into sections with a

Pulling clump apart

Cutting apart and dividing tuberous perennials

sharp, sterile knife. In all cases, cut away any old sections that have died out and replant only the newer, more vigorous sections.

Once your original clump is divided into sections, replant one or two of them into the original location. Take this opportunity to work organic matter into the soil where the perennial was growing before replanting it. The other sections can be moved to new spots in the garden or potted and given away as gifts to gardening friends and neighbours. Get the sections back into the ground as quickly as possible to prevent the exposed roots from drying out. Plan where you are going to plant your divisions and have the spots prepared before you start digging up. Plant your perennial divisions in pots if you aren't sure where to put them all. Water new transplants thoroughly and keep them well watered until they have re-established themselves.

The larger the sections of the division, the more quickly the plant will re-establish itself and grow to blooming size again. For example, a perennial divided into four sections will bloom sooner than one divided into ten sections. Very small divisions may benefit from being planted in pots until they are bigger and better able to fend for themselves in the garden.

Newly planted divisions will need extra care and attention when they are first planted. They will need regular watering and, for the first few days, shade from direct sunlight. A light covering of burlap or damp newspaper should be sufficient to shelter them for this short period. Divisions that have been planted in pots should be moved to a shaded location.

There is some debate about the best time to divide perennials. Some gardeners prefer to divide perennials while they are dormant, whereas others feel perennials establish themselves more quickly if divided when they are growing vigorously. You may wish to experiment with dividing at different times of the year to see what works best for you. If you do divide perennials while they are growing, you will need to cut back one-third to one-half of the growth so as not to stress the roots while they are repairing the damage done to them.

Balloon Flower

PERENNIALS THAT DON'T LIKE DIVISION
Balloon Flower
Euphorbia
Hosta
Japanese Anemone
Lady's Mantle
Oriental Poppy
Peony
Russian Sage

Hosta (above), Peony (below)

PESTS & DISEASES

*P*erennial gardens are both an asset and a liability in terms of pests and diseases. Many insects and diseases attack only one species of plant; it can be difficult for pests and diseases to find their preferred hosts and establish a population in perennial beds containing a mixture of different plant species. At the same time, because the plants are in the same spot for many years, pest problems can become permanent. The advantage is that the beneficial insects, birds and other pest-devouring organisms can also develop permanent populations.

For many years pest control meant spraying or dusting, with the goal to eliminate every pest in the landscape. A more moderate approach advocated today is known as IPM (Integrated Pest Management or Integrated Plant Management). The goal of IPM is to reduce pest problems to levels at which only negligible damage is done. Of course, you, the gardener, must determine what degree of damage is acceptable to you. Consider whether a pest's damage is localized or covers the entire plant. Will the damage being done kill the plant or is it only affecting the outward appearance? Are there methods of controlling the pest without chemicals?

Chemicals are the last resort, because they may do more harm than good. They can endanger the gardener and his or her family and pets, and they kill as many good as bad organisms, leaving the whole garden vulnerable to even worse attacks. A good IPM program includes learning about your plants and the conditions they need for healthy growth, what pests might affect your plants, where and when to look for those pests, and how to control them. Keep records of pest damage because your observations can reveal patterns useful in spotting recurring problems and in planning your maintenance regime.

There are four steps in effective and responsible pest management. Cultural controls are the most important. Physical controls should be attempted next, followed by biological controls. Resort to chemical controls only when the first three possibilities have been exhausted.

Cultural controls are the gardening techniques you use in the day-to-day care of your garden. Keeping your plants as healthy as possible is the best defence against pests. Growing perennials in the conditions they prefer and keeping your soil healthy, with plenty of organic matter, are just two of the cultural controls you can use to keep pests manageable. Choose resistant varieties of perennials that are not prone to problems. Space the plants so that they have good air circulation around them and are not stressed from competing for light, nutrients and space. Remove plants from the landscape if they are decimated by the same pests every year. Remove and burn or take to a permitted dump site diseased foliage and branches, and prevent the spread of disease by keeping your gardening tools clean and by

Tidying up the garden

tidying up fallen leaves and dead plant matter at the end of every growing season.

Physical controls are generally used to combat insect problems. An example of such a control is picking insects off plants by hand, which is not as daunting as it may seem if you catch the problem when it is just beginning. Large, slow insects are particularly easy to pick off. Other physical controls include barriers that stop insects from getting to the plant, and traps that catch or confuse insects. Physical control of diseases often necessitates removing the infected plant part or parts to prevent the spread of the problem.

Bullfrogs eat many insect pests.

Butterflies in the garden add colour and charm.

Biological controls make use of populations of predators that prey on pests. Animals such as birds, snakes, frogs, spiders, lady beetles and certain bacteria can play an important role in keeping pest populations at a manageable level. Encourage these creatures to take up permanent residence in your garden. A birdbath and birdfeeder will encourage birds to enjoy your yard and feed on a wide variety of insect pests. Many beneficial insects are probably already living in your landscape, and you can encourage them to stay by planting appropriate food sources. Many beneficial insects eat nectar from flowers such as yarrow.

Chemical controls should rarely be necessary, but if you must use them there are some 'organic' options available. Organic sprays are no less dangerous than chemical ones, but they will break down into harmless compounds. The main drawback to using any chemicals is that they may also kill the beneficial insects you have been trying to attract to your garden. Organic chemicals are available at most garden centres and you should follow the manufacturer's instructions carefully. A large amount of insecticide is not going to be any more effective in controlling pests than the recommended amount. Note that if a particular pest is not listed on the package, it will not be controlled by that product. Proper and early identification of pests is vital to finding a quick solution.

Whereas cultural, physical, biological and chemical controls are all possible defences against insects, diseases can only be controlled culturally. It is most often weakened plants that succumb to diseases. Healthy plants can often fight off illness, although some diseases can infect plants regardless of their level of health. Prevention is often the only hope: once a plant has been infected, it should probably be destroyed, in order to prevent the disease from spreading.

GLOSSARY OF PESTS & DISEASES

ANTHRACNOSE

Fungus. Yellow or brown spots on leaves; sunken lesions and blisters on stems; can kill plant.

What to Do. Choose resistant varieties and cultivars; keep soil well drained; thin out stems to improve air circulation; avoid handling wet foliage. Remove and destroy infected plant parts; clean up and destroy debris from infected plants at end of growing season.

Larva eating flowers

APHIDS

Tiny, pear-shaped insects, winged or wingless; green, black, brown, red or grey. Cluster along stems, on buds and on leaves. Suck sap from plants; cause distorted or stunted growth. Sticky honeydew forms on surfaces and encourages sooty mould growth.

What to Do. Squish small colonies by hand; brisk water spray dislodges them; many predatory insects and birds feed on them; spray serious infestations with insecticidal soap.

Ladybird beetle larvae (below) are common garden predators.

Aphids on leaf bottom (above)

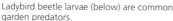

Aesthetic damage from spittlebug (above)
Leaf miner damage (below)

ASTER YELLOWS

Transmitted by insects called leaf-hoppers. Stunted or deformed growth; leaves yellowed and deformed; flowers dwarfed and greenish; can kill plant.
What to Do. Control leafhoppers with insecticidal soap; remove and destroy infected plants; destroy any local weeds sharing the symptoms.

BEETLES

Many types and sizes; usually rounded in shape with hard, shell-like outer wings covering membranous inner wings. Some are beneficial, e.g., ladybird beetles ('ladybugs'); others, e.g., June beetles, eat plants. Larvae: see Borers, Grubs. Leave wide range of chewing damage: make small or large holes in or around margins of leaves; consume entire leaves or areas between leaf veins ('skeletonize'); may also chew holes in flowers.
What to Do. Pick beetles off at night and drop them into an old coffee can half filled with soapy water (soap prevents them from floating); spread an old sheet under plants and shake off beetles to collect and dispose of them.

BORERS

Larvae of some moths, wasps, beetles; among the most damaging plant pests. Burrow into plant stems, branches, leaves and/or roots; destroy vascular tissue (plant veins and arteries) and structural strength. Worm-like; vary in size and get bigger as they bore through plants. Burrow and weaken stems to cause breakage; leaves will wilt; may see tunnels in leaves, stems or roots; rhizomes may be hollowed out entirely or in part.

What to Do. May be able to squish borers within leaves. Remove and destroy bored parts; may need to dig up and destroy infected roots and rhizomes.

BOTRYTIS BLIGHT

Fungal disease. Leaves, stems and flowers blacken, rot and die.

What to Do. Thin stems to improve air circulation, keep mulch away from base of plant, particularly in spring, when plant starts to sprout; remove debris from garden at end of growing season; do not over-water. Remove and destroy any infected plant parts.

BUGS (TRUE BUGS)

Small insects, up to 1 cm (1/2") long; green, brown, black or brightly coloured and patterned. Many beneficial; a few pierce plants to suck out sap. Toxins may be injected that deform plants; sunken areas left

Ladybird Beetle

where pierced; leaves rip as they grow; leaves, buds and new growth may be dwarfed and deformed.

What to Do. Remove debris and weeds from around plants in fall to destroy overwintering sites. Pick off by hand and drop into soapy water; spray plants with insecticidal soap.

Predatory Ground Beetle

Snail eating leaf

CUTWORMS

Larvae of some moths. About 2.5 cm (1") long; plump, smooth-skinned caterpillars; curl up when poked or disturbed. Usually only affect young plants and seedlings, which may be completely consumed or chewed off at ground level.

What to Do. Create physical barriers from old toilet tissue rolls to make collars around plant bases; push tubes at least halfway into ground.

GRUBS

Larvae of different beetles, commonly found below soil level; usually curled in C-shape. Body white or grey; head may be white, grey, brown or reddish. Problematic in lawns; may feed on roots of shallow-rooted trees and shrubs. Plant wilts despite regular watering; may pull easily out of ground in severe cases.

What to Do. Toss any grubs found while digging onto a stone path or patio for birds to devour; apply parasitic nematodes or milky disease spore to infested soil (ask at your local garden centre).

LEAF MINERS

Tiny, stubby larvae of some butterflies and moths; may be yellow or green. Tunnel within leaves leaving winding trails; tunneled areas lighter in colour than rest of leaf. Unsightly rather than health risk to plant.

What to Do. Remove debris from area in fall to destroy overwintering sites; attract parasitic wasps with nectar plants such as yarrow. Remove and destroy infected foliage; can sometimes squish by hand within leaf.

LEAF SPOT

Two common types: one caused by bacteria and the other by fungi. Bacterial: small speckled spots grow to encompass entire leaves; brown or purple in colour; leaves may drop. Fungal: black, brown or yellow spots; leaves wither.

What to Do. Bacterial infection more severe; must remove entire plant. For fungal infection, remove and destroy infected plant parts. Sterilize removal tools; avoid wetting foliage or touching wet foliage; remove and destroy debris at end of growing season.

MEALYBUGS

Tiny crawling insects related to aphids; appear to be covered with white fuzz or flour. Sucking damage stunts and stresses plant. Mealybugs excrete honeydew that promotes growth of sooty mould.

What to Do. Remove by hand on smaller plants; wash plant off with soap and water; wipe off with alcohol-soaked swabs; remove leaves with heavy infestations; encourage or introduce natural predators such as mealybug destroyer beetle and parasitic wasps; spray with insecticidal soap. Keep in mind larvae of mealybug destroyer beetles look like very large mealybugs.

MILDEW

Two types, both caused by fungus, but with slightly different symptoms. Downy mildew: yellow spots on upper sides of leaves and downy fuzz on undersides; fuzz may be yellow, white or grey. Powdery mildew: white or grey powdery coating on leaf surfaces that doesn't brush off.
What to Do. Choose resistant cultivars; space plants well; thin stems to encourage air circulation; tidy any debris in fall. Remove and destroy infected leaves or other parts.

NEMATODES

Tiny worms that give plants disease symptoms. One type infects foliage and stems; the other infects roots. Foliar: yellow spots that turn brown on leaves; leaves shrivel and wither; prob-lem starts on lowest leaves and works up plant. Root-knot: plant is stunted; may wilt; yellow spots on leaves; roots have tiny bumps or knots.
What to Do. Mulch soil, add organic matter, clean up debris in fall. Don't touch wet foliage of infected plants; can add parasitic nematodes to soil. Remove infected plants in extreme cases.

ROT

Several different fungi that affect different parts of the plant and can kill plant. Crown rot: affects base of plant, causing stems to blacken and fall over and leaves to yellow and wilt. Root rot: leaves yellow and plant wilts; digging up plant will show roots rotted away.
What to Do. Keep soil well drained; don't damage plant if you are digging around it; keep mulches away from plant base. Destroy infected plant if whole plant affected.

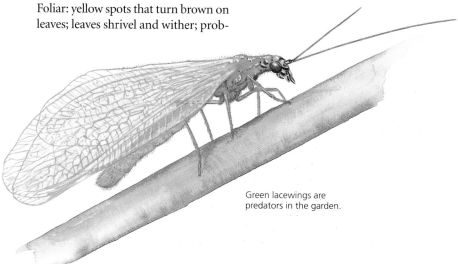

Green lacewings are predators in the garden.

Lygus Bug enjoying annual Cosmos

RUST
Fungi. Pale spots on upper leaf surfaces; orange, fuzzy or dusty spots on leaf undersides.
What to Do. Choose rust-resistant varieties and cultivars; avoid handling wet leaves; provide plant with good air circulation; clear up garden debris at end of season. Remove and destroy infected plant parts.

SLUGS & SNAILS
Slugs lack shells; snails have a spiral shell; both have slimy, smooth skin; can be up to 20 cm (8") long, in Ontario they are smaller, usually no bigger than 4 cm (1.5"); grey, green, black, beige, yellow or spotted. Leave large ragged hole in leaves and silvery slime trails on and around plants.
What to Do. Attach strips of copper to wood around raised beds or smaller boards inserted around susceptible groups of plants; slugs and snails will get shocked if they touch copper surfaces. Pick off by hand in the evening and squish with boot or

drop in can of soapy water. Spread wood ash or diatomaceous earth (available in garden centres) on ground around plants; it will pierce their soft bodies and cause them to dehydrate.

SOOTY MOULD
Fungus. Thin black film forms on leaf surfaces and reduces amount of light getting to leaf surfaces.
What to Do. Wipe mould off leaf surfaces; control insects like aphids, mealybugs, whiteflies (honeydew left on leaves encourages mould).

SPIDER MITES
Almost invisible to the naked eye; relatives of spiders without their insect-eating habits. Tiny; eight-legged; may spin webs; red, yellow or green; usually found on undersides of plant leaves. Suck juice out of leaves; may see fine webbing on leaves and stems; may see mites moving on leaf undersides; leaves become discoloured and speckled in appearance, then turn brown and shrivel up.
What to Do: Wash off with a strong spray of water daily until all signs of infestation are gone; predatory mites are available through garden centres; spray plants with insecticidal soap.

THRIPS
Difficult to see; may be visible if you disturb them by blowing gently on an infested flower. Yellow, black or brown; tiny, slender; narrow fringed wings. Suck juice out of plant cells, particularly in flowers and buds, causing mottled petals and leaves, dying buds and distorted and stunted growth.

What to Do. Remove and destroy infected plant parts; encourage native predatory insects with nectar plants like yarrow; spray severe infestations with insecticidal soap.

VIRUSES

Plant may be stunted and leaves and flowers distorted, streaked or discoloured. Viral diseases in plants cannot be controlled.

What to Do: Destroy infected plants; control insects like aphids, leafhoppers and whiteflies that spread disease.

WHITEFLIES

Tiny flying insects that flutter up into the air when the plant is disturbed. Tiny; moth-like; white; live on undersides of plant leaves. Suck juice out of plant leaves, causing yellowed leaves and weakened plants; leave sticky honeydew on leaves, encouraging sooty mould growth.

What to Do. Destroy weeds where insects may live. Attract native predatory beetles and parasitic wasps with nectar plants like yarrow; spray severe cases with insecticidal soap. Can make a sticky flypaper-like trap by mounting tin can on stake; wrap can with yellow paper and cover with clear baggie smeared with petroleum jelly; replace baggie when full of flies.

WILT

If watering hasn't helped a wilted plant, suspect one of two wilt fungi. *Fusarium* wilt: plant wilts, leaves turn yellow then die; symptoms generally appear first on one part of plant and spread to other parts. *Verticillium* wilt: plant wilts; leaves curl up at edges; leaves turn yellow then drop off; plant may die.

What to Do. Both wilts difficult to control. Choose resistant plant varieties and cultivars; clean up debris at end of growing season. Destroy infected plants; solarize (sterilize) soil before replanting (this may help if you've lost an entire bed of plants to these fungi)—contact local garden centre for assistance.

Harlequin Bugs are another garden predator.

You can make your own insecticidal soap at home. Mix 5 ml (1 tsp.) of mild dish detergent or pure soap (biodegradable options are available) with 1 litre (1 quart) of water in a clean spray bottle. Spray the surface areas of your plants and rinse them well within an hour of spraying.

ABOUT THIS GUIDE

*T*he perennials in this book are organized alphabetically by their common names. Additional common names and Latin names appear after the primary reference. We chose to use local common names instead of the sometimes less familiar scientific names. Later in the text, we describe our favourite recommended or alternate species, but keep in mind that many more hybrids, cultivars and varieties are often available. Check with your local greenhouses or garden centres when making your selection. The Flowers at a Glance section has a small photo of one flower from each entry to allow you to quickly become familiar with the different flowers.

Quick identification information on height, spread, hardiness, flower colour and when to expect the plant to bloom are the first details given on each plant. At the back of the book there is a Quick Reference Chart, a handy guide to planning diversity in your garden. Any particular pests or diseases common to a plant, in any, are noted in each entry. Look in the introduction in the section 'Pests & Diseases' for information on how to solve the problems.

The introduction to the book outlines three main climate regions in Ontario and where you can expect hardy, semi-hardy and tender perennials to do well. A corresponding map will allow you to determine the general growing conditions in your part of the province. The introduction also includes information on selecting, caring for and propagating perennials.

The Perennials

Ajuga
Bugleweed
Ajuga

Height: 10–30 cm (4–12") **Spread:** 45 cm (18"), or wider
Flower colour: purple, blue, pink, white; grown for foliage
Blooms: late spring to early summer **Hardiness:** hardy

*M*any groundcovers do a serviceable job of blanketing the ground, but cultivars of ajuga have the added benefit of producing abundant blue flowers in spring. Wisely chosen spring bulbs, such as crocuses and miniature daffodils, can combine beautifully with this vigorous plant.

PLANTING
Seeding: Not recommended. Foliage often reverts to green in seedlings.
Planting out: Any time of year.
Spacing: 30–45 cm (12–18") apart.

In the past a syrup made from ajuga was used to cure hangovers.

GROWING

Ajuga plants will grow in any light from **full sun** to **full shade**. Best foliage colour develops in **partial or light shade**. Any **well-drained** soil is suitable. Divide these vigorous plants any time during the growing season.

TIPS

Ajugas make excellent groundcovers for difficult sites, such as exposed slopes and dense shade. They are also attractive groundcovers in shrub borders, where the dense growth of the ajugas will prevent the spread of all but the most tenacious weeds.

Ajugas can easily take over the lawn because they readily spread by stolons (above-ground shoots) and their low growth form escapes the lawn-mower blades. The spread of ajugas may be somewhat controlled by the use of bed-edging materials. If an ajuga starts to take over, it is easy to rip out, and the soil it leaves behind will be soft and loose from the penetrating roots. Use an ajuga as a scout plant to send ahead and prepare the soil before you plant anything more particular in a shaded or woodland garden.

Any new growth or seedlings that don't show the hybrid leaf colouring should be removed.

A. reptans

Bugleweed is widely used in homeopathic remedies for throat and mouth irritations.

A. reptans

A. reptans

RECOMMENDED

A. reptans is a low, quick-spreading groundcover. This species is almost never grown in favour of the many attractive cultivars. **'Braunherz'** is an excellent, fairly new, purple-bronze cultivar. It is compact and richly coloured all year. **'Burgundy Glow'** has foliage variegated in shades of bronze, green, white and pink. The habit is dense and compact. **'Caitlin's Giant'** has large, bronze leaves. It bears short spikes of bright blue flowers in spring. **'Multicolor'** ('Rainbow,' 'Tricolor') is a vigorous spreader. The bronze leaves are splashed with pink and white. **'Royalty'** is a new form with dark purple foliage and contrasting bright purple-blue flowers. **'Variegata'** is dense and slow growing. The green leaves have silver margins. The best colour develops in the shade.

According to European folk myths, bugleweed causes fires if brought into the house.

A. reptans

ALTERNATE SPECIES

A. genevensis (Geneva Bugleweed) is an upright, non-invasive species. The spring flowers are blue, white or pink. It grows 15–30 cm (6–12") tall and spreads 45 cm (18"). This species is more suitable in a rock garden or near a lawn because it will not take over in the way *A. reptans* is likely to do.

PROBLEMS & PESTS

Occasional problems with crown rot, leaf spot and root rot can be avoided by providing good air circulation and by making sure the plant is not standing in water for extended periods.

'Burgundy Glow'

'Caitlin's Giant'

Anemone
Windflower
Anemone

Height: 8–150 cm (3–60") **Spread:** 15–60 cm (6–24")
Flower colour: white, yellow, pink, blue **Blooms:** spring, summer or fall
Hardiness: hardy, semi-hardy

Gardeners should pay more attention to the lovely anemones. Grecian Windflower, with a short blooming period but a big impact, is a pure delight in the spring garden. Japanese Anemone is an attractive plant at all stages and deserves to be planted in all gardens. It puts on vegetative growth during summer, gassing up the reserves for a prolonged fall show. Suddenly when other plants are bedraggled and bug bitten, Japanese Anemone starts opening its white or pink flowers on tall, strong stems. In my garden this display goes on for weeks and never fails to impress gardeners unfamiliar with the charms of Japanese Anemone. Be patient—this variety may take a while to get established.

PLANTING

Seeding: Not recommended.
Planting out: Spring.
Spacing: 10–45 cm (4–18") apart.

GROWING

Anemones prefer **partial or light shade** and tolerate full sun. Soil should be of **average to high fertility, humus rich** and **moist**. *A. blanda* prefers a
light, sandy soil. While dormant, anemones prefer
to have dry soil. Mulch Japanese Anemone the
first winter to help it get established. Divide in
spring or fall. Grecian Windflower prefers to be
divided in summer.

TIPS

Anemones make a beautiful addition to lightly
shaded borders, woodland gardens and rock
gardens.

RECOMMENDED

A. blanda (Grecian Windflower) is a low, spreading, tuberous perennial that bears blue flowers in
spring. It grows 15–20 cm (6–8") tall, with an
equal spread. **'White Splendor'** is a vigorous plant
with white flowers. **'Pink Star'** has pink flowers
with yellow centres.

A. x hybrida

*The name of the
Anemone comes from
the Greek anemos,
meaning 'wind.'
The plant grows on
windswept mountain-
sides, which is how it
got its name.*

'White Splendor'

'Whirlwind'

A. *canadensis* (Meadow Anemone) is a spreading perennial with slightly invasive tendencies. It grows 30–60 cm (12–24") tall, with an equal spread. The yellow-centered, white flowers are borne in late spring and early summer. This plant needs regular watering when first planted to become established.

A. x *hybrida* (Japanese Anemone) is an upright, suckering perennial. It grows 60–150 cm (24–60") tall, spreads about 60 cm (24") and bears pink or white flowers from late summer to mid-fall. There are numerous cultivars available. **'Max Vogel'** has large pink flowers. **'Honorine Jobert'** has plentiful white flowers. **'Pamina'** has pinkish-red double flowers. **'Whirlwind'** has semi-double white flowers.

'White Giant'

A. nemerosa (Wood Anemone) is a low, creeping perennial. It grows 7.5–25 cm (3–10") tall and spreads 30 cm (12") or more. The spring flowers are white, often flushed with pink. **'Flore Pleno'** has double white flowers. **'Rosea'** has red-purple flowers.

PROBLEMS & PESTS

The rare, but possible, problems include leaf gall, downy mildew, smut, fungal leaf spot, powdery mildew, rust, nematodes, caterpillars, slugs and flea beetles.

A. x hybrida

A. x hybrida

Artemisia
Wormwood, Sage
Artemisia

Height: 15–180 cm (6–72") **Spread:** 30–90 cm (12–36")
Flower colour: white or yellow, generally inconspicuous; foliage plant
Blooms: late summer **Hardiness:** hardy, semi-hardy

New gardeners may not see the reason to plant this foliage plant that never flowers. But as the garden and gardener mature, the charm of artemisias is revealed. They are perfect plants for cooling down hot colours—think of an artemisia as a mediator between hotheads. The silver-grey foliage also acts as a blender, helping to knit together drifts of other perennials. I have 'Valerie Finnis' planted with tall Bearded Iris, and it is an effective combination.

PLANTING

Seeding: Not recommended.
Planting out: Spring, summer or fall.
Spacing: 25–90 cm (10–36").

GROWING

Artemisias grow best in **full sun**. Soil should be of **average to high fertility** and **well drained**. They dislike wet, humid conditions. Artemisia plants respond well to pruning in late spring. If you prune before May, frost may kill any new growth. Whenever artemisias begin to look straggly they may be cut back hard to encourage new growth and maintain a neater form. Some species can become invasive. Division can be done every one or two years when plants appear to be thinning in the centres.

'Nana'

A. ludoviciana

TIPS

Artemisias can be used in rock gardens and borders. The silver-grey foliage makes these good backdrop plants behind brightly coloured flowers, and they are useful for filling in the spaces between other plants. Smaller forms may also be used to create knot gardens.

If you want to control horizontal spreading of an artemisia, plant it in a bottomless container. Sunk into the ground, the container is hidden and it will prevent the plant from spreading beyond the container's edges. With the bottom missing, good drainage can also be maintained.

RECOMMENDED

A. absinthium (Common Wormwood) is a clump-forming, woody-based perennial. It has aromatic, hairy, grey foliage and bears inconspicuous yellow flowers in late summer. It grows 60–90 cm (24–36") tall and spreads about 60 cm (24"). **'Lambrook Silver'** has attractive silver-grey foliage.

A. lactiflora (White Mugwort) is an upright, clump-forming perennial. This is one of the few artemisias to bear showy flowers. It grows 120–180 cm (48–72") tall and spreads 60–90 cm (24–36"). The foliage is dark green or grey-green.

'Nana'

Attractive creamy-white flowers are borne from late summer to mid-fall.

A. ludoviciana (White Sage, Western Mugwort) is an upright, clump-forming perennial. It grows 60–120 cm (24–48") tall and spreads 60 cm (24"). The foliage is silvery white and the flowers are inconspicuous. The species is not grown as often as the cultivars. **'Valerie Finnis'** is a good choice for hot, dry areas. It has very wide, silvery leaves, is less invasive than the species, and combines beautifully with many other perennials. **'Silver King'** is compact and very hardy. It has very hairy, silvery-white foliage. It grows about 60 cm (24") tall. **'Silver Queen'** has deeply divided, silvery foliage. It can be invasive. It grows 60–75 cm (24–30") tall.

***A.* 'Powis Castle'** is compact, mounding and shrubby. It grows 60–90 cm (24–36") tall, with an equal spread. It has feathery, silver-grey foliage and inconspicuous flowers. This cultivar is only semi-hardy.

A. schmidtiana (Silvermound) is a low, dense, mound-forming perennial. It grows 30–60 cm (12–24") tall and spreads 30–45 cm (12–18"). The foliage is feathery, hairy and silvery grey. **'Nana'** (Dwarf Silvermound) is very compact and grows only half the size of the species.

PROBLEMS & PESTS

Rust, downy mildew and fungal problems are possible.

There are almost 300 species of Artemisia throughout the world.

There are two possible sources of the genus name: it quite possibly honours the botanist and medical researcher from 353 BC, Artemisia, who was the sister of King Mausolus; the other possibility is that it was named after Artemis, the Goddess of the Hunt and the Moon of Greek mythology.

A. lactiflora

Aster

Aster

Height: 25–150 cm (10–60") **Spread:** 45–90 cm (18–36")
Flower colour: red, white, blue, purple, pink
Blooms: late summer to mid-fall **Hardiness:** hardy, semi-hardy

*T*hese perennials often get bypassed in the frantic spring shopping season, but they shouldn't. Asters deliver the goods in late summer and fall when a garden's design deficiencies can show up. The purples and pinks of asters make a nice contrast to the yellow-flowered perennials common in the late-summer garden.

PLANTING

Seeding: Not recommended.
Planting out: Spring or fall.
Spacing: 45–90 cm (18–36").

GROWING

Asters prefer **full sun** but tolerate partial shade. Soil should be **fertile, moist** and **well drained.** Pinching or shearing these plants back in early summer will promote dense growth and reduce disease problems. A winter mulch will protect them from temperature fluctuations. Divide every two to three years to maintain vigour and control spread.

TIPS

Asters can be used in the middle of borders and in cottage gardens. These plants can also be naturalized in wild gardens.

A. novi-belgii

This old-fashioned flower was once called starwort because of the many petals that radiate out from the centre.

A. novi-belgii

*What looks like a
single flower on a
Michaelmas daisy,
or other daisy-like
plants, is actually a
cluster of many tiny
flowers. Look closely
at the centre of the
flowerhead and you
will see all the tiny
individual flowers.*

RECOMMENDED

A. x *frikartii* will bloom in light to dark shades of
purple nonstop and abundantly. These hybrids
like a well-drained spot and can be temperamen-
tal. They may need re-planting after several years.
They grow up to 60 cm (24") tall and spread to 45
cm (18"). **'Mönch'** is a taller variety, up to 75 cm
(30"), with abundant lavender blue flowers.

A. *novae-angliae* (Michaelmas Daisy, New England Aster) is an upright, spreading, clump-
forming perennial. It grows to 150 cm (60") tall
and spreads to 60 cm (24"). From late summer to
mid-fall it bears yellow-centered, purple flowers.
'Purple Dome' is dwarf and spreading with dark
purple flowers. This cultivar is mildew resistant.

A. novae-angliae

It grows 45–60 cm (18–24") tall and spreads 60–75 cm (24–30"). **'Alma Potschke'** bears bright salmon pink or cherry red flowers. It grows 90–120 cm (36–48") tall and spreads 60 cm (24").

A. novi-belgii (Michaelmas Daisy, New York Aster) is a dense, upright, clump-forming perennial. It grows 90–120 cm (36–48") tall and spreads 45–90 cm (18–36"). **'Chequers'** is a compact plant with purple flowers. **'Alice Haslam'** is a dwarf plant with bright pink flowers. It grows 25–45 cm (10–18") tall and spreads 45 cm (18").

PROBLEMS & PESTS
Powdery mildew, aster wilt, aster yellows, aphids, mites, slugs and nematodes can cause trouble.

A. novi-belgii

A. novi-belgii

Astilbe

Astilbe

Height: 25–120 cm (10–48") **Spread:** 20–90 cm (8–36")
Flower colour: white, pink, purple, peach, red
Blooms: early, mid- or late summer, depending on the cultivar
Hardiness: hardy

*A*stilbes are the saviours of the shady garden. Their high-impact flowers of white, pink and red brighten up any gloomy section of the garden. Because so many people garden in shade, hybridizers continue to develop this perennial. There are many choices now in colour, leaf habit and size and blooming time.

In late summer, transplant seedlings found near the parent plant for plumes of colour throughout the garden.

PLANTING

Seeding: Not recommended; seedlings do not come true to type.
Planting out: Spring.
Spacing: 45–90 cm (18–36") apart.

GROWING

Astilbes enjoy **light or partial shade** and tolerate full shade, though with reduced flowering in deep shade. Soil should be **fertile, humus rich, acidic, moist** and **well drained**. Astilbes like to grow near water sources, such as ponds and streams, but they dislike standing in water. Provide a mulch in summer to keep the roots cool and moist. Divide every three years in spring or fall to maintain plant vigour.

A. x arendsii

A. x arendsii

TIPS

Astilbes can be grown near the edges of bog gardens or ponds and in woodland gardens and shaded borders.

The root crown of an astilbe tends to lift out of the soil as the plant grows bigger. This problem can be solved by applying a top dressing of rich soil as a mulch when the plant starts lifting or by lifting the entire plant and replanting it deeper into the soil.

Astilbe flowers fade to various shades of brown. The flowers may be removed once flowering is finished or they may be left in place.

Astilbes self-seed easily and the flowerheads look interesting and natural in the garden well into fall.

RECOMMENDED

A. x *arendsii* (Astilbe, False Spirea) grows 45–120 cm (18–48") tall and spreads 45–90 cm (18–36"). There are many cultivars available from this hybrid group. The following are a few popular ones. **'Avalanche'** bears white flowers in late summer. **'Bressingham Beauty'** bears bright pink flowers in mid-summer. **'Cattleya'** bears reddish-pink flowers in mid-summer. **'Fanal'** bears red flowers in early summer and has deep bronze foliage. **'Weisse Gloria'** bears creamy white flowers in mid- to late summer.

A. x arendsii

A. chinensis (Chinese Astilbe) is a dense, vigorous perennial that is more tolerant of dry soil than other astilbe species. It grows about 60 cm (24") tall and spreads 45 cm (18"). It bears fluffy white, pink or purple flowers in late summer. **Var.** *pumila* is more commonly found than the species. This plant forms a low groundcover with dark pink flowers. It grows 25 cm (10") tall and spreads 20 cm (8"). **'Superba'** is a tall form with lavender purple flowers produced in a long narrow spike.

A. japonica (Japanese Astilbe) is a compact, clump-forming perennial. The species is rarely grown in favour of the cultivars. **'Etna'** grows 60–75 cm (24–30") tall and spreads 45–60 cm (18–24"). It bears dark red flowers in early summer. **'Deutschland'** grows 50 cm (20") tall and spreads 30 cm (12"). It bears white flowers in late spring.

PROBLEMS & PESTS

A variety of pests can on occasion attack astilbes. Powdery mildew, bacterial leaf spot and fungal leaf spot are also possible problems.

'Bressingham Beauty'

Astilbes are great as cut flowers and if you leave the plumes in a vase as the water evaporates, you'll have dried flowers to enjoy all winter.

'Deutschland'

88

Balloon Flower

Platycodon

Height: 60–90 cm (24–36") **Spread:** 30–45 cm (12–18")
Flower colour: blue, pink, white **Blooms:** summer
Hardiness: hardy

Recapture the joy of childhood by growing Balloon Flower. When pumped up and full of air just before blooming, the buds look like tiny balloons. You'll be tempted to squeeze the buds to open the simple star-shaped flowers of lovely clear blue. Balloon Flower can tend to flop, so I pinch back about half of the shoots in early summer to shorten the stems and delay some of the blossoms.

PLANTING

Seeding: Start indoors in late winter or direct sow spring. Blooms second year after seeding.
Planting out: Spring.
Spacing: 30–45 cm (12–18") apart.

GROWING

Balloon Flower grows well in **full sun** or **partial shade**. Soil should be of **average to rich fertility, light, moist** and **well drained**. Balloon Flower dislikes wet soil. This plant sprouts late in the year. To avoid accidentally damaging it, be sure to mark where you put it. Propagate by gently detaching the side shoots that sprout up around the plant. Plants will self-seed and the seedlings can be moved to new locations, if desired. Balloon Flower rarely needs dividing. It resents having its roots disturbed and can take a long time to re-establish itself after dividing.

P. grandiflorus var. *albus*

TIPS

Use Balloon Flower in borders, rock gardens and cottage gardens.

Pinch off spent flowers to improve appearance.

RECOMMENDED

P. grandiflorus is an upright, clump-forming perennial, though the cultivars tend to be lower and more rounded in habit. It grows 60–90 cm (24–36") tall and spreads 30–45 cm (12–18") and bears blue flowers in summer. **Var.** *albus* bears white flowers, often veined with blue. **'Mother of Pearl'** bears pale pink flowers. **'Double Blue'** is a compact plant with purple-blue, double flowers. **'Fuji Blue'** from Japan has deep blue flowers, excellent for cutting. **'Fuji Pink'** bears clear pink flowers. **'Sentimental Blue'** is a new dwarf form with intense blue flowers, good for containers.

When using these flowers in arrangements it is advisable to singe the cut ends with a lit match to prevent the milky white sap from running.

Basket-of-Gold

Aurinia

Height: 15–45 cm (6–18") **Spread:** 20–45 cm (8–18")
Flower colour: yellow or occasionally apricot
Blooms: mid-spring **Hardiness:** hardy

W hen spring is still cool and most plants are just beginning to peek out of the soil, this electric-yellow perennial comes into full bloom. Basket-of-gold warms us up, quickly filling its corner of the garden with a bright spring glow. Combine with vigorous rock garden plants and spring bulbs such as tulips, but be careful if you plant it with slow-growing alpine plants because it can quickly overwhelm them.

PLANTING

Seeding: Sow seeds in containers in cold frame in spring.
Planting out: Early to mid-spring.
Spacing: 30–45 cm (12–18") apart.

GROWING

Basket-of-gold prefers **full sun**. Soil should be of **average to poor fertility, sandy** and **well drained**. Basket-of-gold can rot in wet soil, and growth becomes floppy in rich soil. It is drought tolerant. Shearing Basket-of-gold back lightly after flowering will keep the plant compact and will occasionally encourage a few more flowers. Do not shear off all flowerheads in hot regions, as the plants do not live as long when exposed to high temperatures. Self-seeding will provide new plants once the old ones die. Cuttings can be taken from the new growth that emerges after flowering. Established plants should not be moved or divided.

Basket-of-gold belongs to the Brassica family, which includes such plants as cabbage and broccoli.

TIPS

Use in borders and rock gardens, along wall tops and as a ground-cover in difficult or little-used areas.

Avoid planting Basket-of-gold near slow-growing plants because it can quickly choke them out.

RECOMMENDED

A. saxatilis is a vigorous, mound-forming perennial. It grows 20–30 cm (8–12") tall and spreads 30–45 cm (12–18") or more. It bears bright yellow flowers in mid-spring. **'Citrina'** bears light, lemon yellow flowers. **'Compacta'** bears golden yellow

flowers. It is a bit smaller than the species, growing about 15 cm (6") tall and spreading 20 cm (8"). **'Dudley Nevill'** bears apricot-coloured flowers. **'Gold Ball'** is a clump-forming plant with bright yellow flowers held above the foliage. **'Variegata'** bears lemon yellow flowers and has irregular cream-coloured margins on the foliage.

PROBLEMS & PESTS
Basket-of-gold generally has no serious problems but can rot in wet soil.

Cuttings can be taken from the new growth that starts after the spent flowerheads are sheared back.

Beard Tongue

Penstemon

Height: 45–150 cm (18–60") **Spread:** 30–60 cm (12–24")
Flower colour: white, yellow, pink, purple, red
Blooms: spring, summer, fall **Hardiness:** hardy

*T*here is great diversity in this group of plants—the flowers can be a shy, pale pink or flaming orange. Some penstemons will re-seed in the garden, and others will disappear. They are mostly natives of North America. With the wide range now available, they should find a home in every perennial garden.

PLANTING

Seeding: Start indoors in late summer or early spring. Soil temperature at 13–18° C (55–64° F).
Planting out: Spring or fall.
Spacing: 30–60 cm (12–24").

GROWING

Beard tongue prefers **full sun** but tolerates partial shade. Soil should be of **average to rich fertility** and **well drained**. These plants can rot in wet soil and are drought tolerant. Mulch in winter to protect from cold. Pinch plants when they are 30 cm (12") tall to encourage bushy growth. Divide every two to three years in spring.

TIPS

Use in a mixed or herbaceous border, a cottage garden or rock garden.

Twiggy branches pushed into the ground around young beard tongue plants will provide them with support as they grow.

There are over 200 species of Penstemon *found native in varied habitats from mountains to open plains throughout North and South America.*

RECOMMENDED

P. 'Alice Hindley' bears pinkish-purple flowers with white throats from mid-summer to fall. It grows 60–90 cm (24–36") tall and spreads 30–45 cm (12–18")

P. 'Apple Blossom' bears pink-flushed white flowers. This rounded perennial grows 45–60 cm (18–24") tall, with an equal width.

P. barbatus is an upright, rounded perennial. It grows 45–90 cm (18–36") tall and spreads 30–45 cm (12–18"). Red or pink flowers are borne from early summer to early fall. **'Praecox Nanus'** ('Nanus Rondo') is a compact, dwarf plant that grows about half the size of the species. It bears pink, purple or red flowers. **'Alba'** has white flowers.

P. digitalis (Foxglove Penstemon) is a very hardy, upright, semi-evergreen perennial. It grows 60–150 cm (24–60") tall and spreads 45–60 cm (18–24"). It bears white flowers, often veined with purple, all summer. **'Husker Red'** has red stems and red-purple new foliage and is good for mass planting. This was a perennial plant of the year in 1996, as selected by the Perennial Plant Association. The flowers are white and veined with red.

P. **'Elfin Pink'** is very reliable and has compact spikes of clear pink.

P. **'Hyacinth Mix'** is a hardy seed strain producing flowers in a mix of pink, lilac, blue and scarlet.

P. **'Prairie Dusk'** has tall spikes of tubular rose-purple flowers; it blooms over a long season.

P. **'White Bedder'** grows 60–75 cm (34–30") tall and 45 cm (18") wide. Its white flowers become pink tinged and bloom from mid-summer to mid-autumn.

PROBLEMS & PESTS

Powdery mildew, rust and leaf spot can occur, but are rarely serious problems.

P. 'White Bedder'

Bellflower

Campanula

Height: 10–180 cm (4–72") **Spread:** 30–90 cm (12–36")
Flower colour: blue, white, purple, pink
Blooms: spring, summer **Hardiness:** hardy

I've been remiss in not using more bellflowers in the garden. These perennials are so diverse, entire books are now devoted to their charms. You can select bellflowers ranging from the tiniest creeper to tall, stately back-of-the-border plants. *Campanula carpatica* is often used as an edging plant; it blooms abundantly and faithfully. The cultivar 'Kent Belle,' with large blue flowers, is making a big impact with perennial lovers.

PLANTING

Seeding: Not recommended. Direct sow in spring or fall. Germination can be erratic.
Planting out: Spring or fall.
Spacing: 30–90 cm (12–36").

GROWING

Bellflowers grow well in **full sun, partial shade** or **light shade**. Soil should be of **average to high fertility** and **well drained**. Bellflowers appreciate summer mulch to keep their roots cool, and a winter mulch is beneficial, especially if snow cover is inconsistent.

Bellflowers respond well to deadheading to prolong blooming. Use scissors to cut back one-third of the plant at a time, allowing other sections to continue blooming. As the pruned section starts to bud, cut back other sections for continued blooming. It is important to divide bellflowers every few years in early spring or late summer to keep plants vigorous and to prevent them from becoming invasive.

C. carpatica

C. persicifolia

C. 'Birch Hybrid'

Bellflower can be propagated by basal, new-growth or rhizome cuttings.

C. persicifolia

TIPS

Low, spreading and trailing bellflowers can be used in rock gardens and on rock walls. Upright and mounding bellflowers can be used in borders and cottage gardens. You can also edge beds with the low-growing varieties.

RECOMMENDED

C. **'Birch Hybrid'** is low growing and spreading. It bears light blue to mauve flowers in summer.

C. carpatica (Carpathian Bellflower, Carpathian Harebell) is a spreading, mounding perennial. It grows 25–30 cm (10–12") tall and spreads 30–60 cm (12–24") and bears blue, white or purple flowers in summer. **'Blue Clips'** is a smaller, compact plant with large blue flowers. **'Bressingham White'** is a compact plant with large white flowers. **'Jewel'** is low growing with deep blue flowers. It grows 10–20 cm (4–8") tall. **'Kent Belle'** is a stately new hybrid with large, deep violet-blue bells on arching stems.

C. lactiflora (Milky Bellflower) is an upright perennial. It grows 120–180 cm (48–72") tall and spreads about 60 cm (24"). Summer flowers are white, light to dark blue, or light to dark purple. **Var. *alba*** ('Alba') bears white flowers.

C. persicifolia (Peach-Leaved Bellflower) is an upright perennial. It grows about 90 cm (36") tall and spreads about 30 cm (12"). It bears white, blue or purple flowers from early summer to mid-summer.

C. portenschlagiana (Dalmation Bellflower) is a low, spreading, mounding perennial. It grows 15 cm (6") tall and spreads 50–60 cm (20–24"). It bears light or deep purple flowers from mid- to late summer.

C. 'Birch Hybrid'

C. poscharskyana (Serbian Bellflower) is a trailing perennial. It grows 15–30 cm (6–12") tall and spreads 60–90 cm (24–36"). It bears light purple flowers in summer and early fall.

PROBLEMS & PESTS

Minor problems with vine weevils, spider mites, aphids, powdery mildew, slugs, rust and fungal leaf spot are possible.

There are over 300 species of Campanula *found throughout the Northern Hemisphere in habitats ranging from high rocky crags to boggy meadows.*

C. poscharskyana

Bergamot
Bee Balm
Monarda

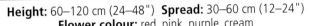

Height: 60–120 cm (24–48") **Spread:** 30–60 cm (12–24")
Flower colour: red, pink, purple, cream
Blooms: summer **Hardiness:** hardy

*I*f it is in a happy spot in the garden, Bergamot will form a high-impact clump of flowers in red, pink or salmon. Each flower is a visual delight, sure to bring a smile to your face and bees and butterflies to your garden. Hybridizers continue to work on mildew-resistant varieties.

This plant is named after the Spanish botanist and physician Nicholas Monardes (1493–1588).

PLANTING

Seeding: Start seeds outdoors in cold frame or indoors in early spring.
Planting out: Spring or fall.
Spacing: 45–60 cm (18–24") apart.

GROWING

Bergamot grows well in **full sun, partial shade** or **full shade**. Soil should be of **average fertility, humus rich, moist** and **well drained.** Divide every two or three years in spring before new growth emerges.

TIPS

Use Bergamot beside a stream or pond, or in a lightly shaded, well-watered border.

Bergamot will attract bees, butterflies and hummingbirds to your garden. Avoid using pesticides that can seriously harm or kill these creatures especially if you plan to ingest this, or any plant, in your garden.

M. 'Cambridge Scarlet'

The fresh or dried leaves may be used to make a refreshing, minty, citrus-scented tea. Put a handful of fresh leaves in a teapot, pour boiling water over the leaves and let steep for at least five minutes. Sweeten the tea with honey to suit your own taste.

The common name, Bergamot, comes from the scent of the Italian Bergamot orange (Citrus bergamia) *often used in aromatherapy.*

RECOMMENDED

M. didyma is a bushy, mounding plant that forms a thick clump of stems. It grows 60–120 cm (24–48") tall and spreads 30–60 cm (12–24"). Red or pink flowers are borne in late summer. **'Cambridge Scarlet'** bears bright scarlet-red flowers. **'Gardenview Scarlet'** bears large scarlet flowers and is resistant to powdery mildew. **'Marshall's Delight'** doesn't come true to type from seed and must be propagated by cuttings or divisions. It is very resistant to powdery mildew and bears pink flowers. **'Panorama'** is a group of hybrids with flowers in scarlet, pink or salmon.

PROBLEMS & PESTS

Powdery mildew is the worst problem, but rust, leaf spot and leaf hoppers can cause trouble. To help prevent powdery mildew, thin the stems in spring. If mildew strikes after flowering, cut the plants back to 15 cm (6") to increase air circulation. Don't allow the plant to dry out for extended periods.

M. 'Cambridge Scarlet'

Bergenia

Bergenia

Height: 30–60 cm (12–24") **Spread:** 45–60 cm (18–24")
Flower colour: red, purple, dark to light pink, white
Blooms: early spring **Hardiness:** hardy

Bergenias surprise the gardener. I planted a bergenia in what I thought was a perfect spot, in semi-shade with good soil. It did not do well. I consigned it to what I thought was plant purgatory by planting it in 25 cm (10") of soil on top of cement blocks. There it has flourished. Cold-climate gardeners like these plants because they are evergreen. In winter the glossy leaves take on a red-bronze luster. Plant in masses, and look forward to bright pink flowers in early spring.

PLANTING

Seeding: Seed may not come true to type. Fresh, ripe seeds should be sown uncovered. Keep soil temperature at 20–21° C (69–70° F).
Planting out: Spring.
Spacing: 25–50 cm (10–20").

GROWING

Bergenias grow well in **full sun** or **partial shade**. Soil should be of **average to rich fertility** and **well drained**. A moist soil is preferable, but plants are drought tolerant once established.

Propagating by seed can be somewhat risky. You may not get what you hoped for. A more certain way to get more of the plants you have is to propagate them with root cuttings. Bergenias spread just below the surface by rhizomes, which may be cut off in pieces and grown separately as long as a leaf shoot is attached to the section. Divide every two to three years when the clump begins to die out in the middle.

TIPS

These versatile, low-growing, spreading plants can be used as groundcovers, to edge borders and pathways, in rock gardens and in mass plantings under trees and shrubs.

Another common name for this plant is elephant ears because of the large leathery leaves.

Once flowering is complete, in early spring, bergenias still make a beautiful addition to the garden with their thick, leathery, glossy leaves. A bergenia plant provides a soothing background for other flowers with its expanse of green. As well, many varieties turn attractive colours of bronze and purple in fall and winter.

RECOMMENDED
B. **'Bressingham White'** grows about 30 cm (12") tall and has white flowers.

B. ciliata (Winter 45–60 cm (18–24" equal spread. Its fl light pink.

B. cordifolia (Heart Bergenia) grows about 60 c with an equal or greater spread. wers are deep pink, and the foliage rns bronze or purple in fall and winter. **'Purpurea'** has magenta-purple flowers and red-tinged foliage.

B. x *schmidtii*

B. x *schmidtii*

B. 'Evening Glow' ('Abdënglut') grows about 30 cm (12") tall and spreads 45–60 cm (18–24") wide. The flowers are a deep magenta-crimson. The foliage turns red and maroon in the winter.

B. x *schmidtii* is a compact plant that grows 30 cm (12") tall and spreads 60 cm (24"). The flowers are pink.

B. 'Winter Fairy Tale' ('Wintermärchen') grows 30–45 cm (12–18") tall and spreads 45–60 cm (18–24"). The flowers are rose red, and the dark green leaves are touched with red in winter.

PROBLEMS & PESTS

Rare problems with slugs, fungal leaf spot, root rot, weevils, caterpillars and foliar nematodes are possible.

Black-Eyed Susan
Rudbeckia

Height: 45–300 cm (18–120") **Spread:** 30–90 cm (12–36")
Flower colour: yellow, orange, red, with brown or green centres
Blooms: mid-summer to fall **Hardiness:** hardy

Very few plants re-seed in my hot, dry, nutrient-poor garden, but the black-eyed Susans do. New gardeners and those with lots of bare soil to plant should put the *Rudbeckia* group at the top of their lists. The various forms of black-eyed Susans are tough, drought-tolerant North American natives. They bloom diligently for weeks from mid-summer onward.

PLANTING

Seeding: Start seed in cold frame or indoors in early spring. Soil temperature at about 16–18° C (61–64° F).
Planting out: Spring.
Spacing: 30–90 cm (12–36") apart.

GROWING

Black-eyed Susans grow well in **full sun** or **partial shade**. Soil should be of **average fertility** and **well drained**. A **fairly heavy** clay soil is preferred. Regular watering is best, but established plants are drought tolerant. Pinching plants in June will make shorter, bushier stands. Divide in spring or fall every three to five years.

TIPS

Use black-eyed Susans in a wildflower or naturalistic garden, in borders and in cottage-style gardens. They are best planted in masses and drifts.

RECOMMENDED

R. fulgida is an upright, spreading plant. It grows 45–90 cm (18–36") tall and spreads 30–60 cm (12–24"). The orange-yellow flowers have brown centres. **Var.** *sullivantii* **'Goldsturm'** bears large, bright yellow flowers.

R. laciniata (Cutleaf Coneflower) forms a large, open clump. It grows 1.2–3 m (4–10') tall and spreads 60–90 cm (24–36"). The yellow flowers have green centres. The cultivar **'Goldquelle'** grows 90 cm (36") tall and has bright yellow, double flowers.

R. nitida is an upright, spreading plant. It grows 90–180 cm (36–72") tall and spreads 60–90 cm (24–36"). The yellow flowers have green centres. **'Autumn Glory'** has golden yellow flowers. **'Herbstsonne'** ('Autumn Sun') has bright yellow flowers.

PROBLEMS & PESTS

Rare problems with slugs, aphids, rust, smut and leaf spot are possible.

R. fulgida

Black-eyed Susan flowers are long-lasting in cut arrangements.

R. fulgida

Blazing Star
Spike Gayfeather; Gayfeather
Liatris

Height: 45–90 cm (18–36") **Spread:** 45–60 cm (18–24")
Flower colour: purple, white
Blooms: summer **Hardiness**: hardy

When Blazing Star is blooming contentedly in the garden, it is easy to take it for granted. Remember that in winter when you are buying it as a cut flower from the florist at a handsome price. Blazing Star is an outstanding cut flower with its fuzzy, spiked blossoms above grass-like foliage. It is also an excellent plant for attracting butterflies to the garden.

PLANTING

Seeding: Direct sow in fall. Plants may take two to four years to bloom from seed.
Planting out: Spring.
Spacing: 45–60 cm (18–24") apart.

GROWING

Blazing Star prefers **full sun**. Soil should be of **average fertility, sandy** and **humus rich**. Water well during the growing season, but don't allow the plants to stand in water during cool weather. Mulch during summer to prevent moisture loss. Trim off the spent flower spikes to promote a longer blooming period and to keep the plants looking tidy. Divide every three or four years in fall. The clump will appear crowded when it is time to divide.

L. spicata

TIPS

Use these plants in bog gardens, borders and meadow plantings. Blazing Star doesn't like to sit in water during cool weather and may develop root rot during winter. Plant in a location that has good drainage. Blazing Star does well when grown in planters.

RECOMMENDED

L. spicata is an erect, clump-forming plant. It grows 60–90 cm (24–36") tall and spreads 45–60 cm (18–24"). The flowers are pinkish purple or white. **'Floristan Violet'** has purple flowers. **'Floristan White'** has white flowers. **'Kobold'** has deep purple flowers.

PROBLEMS & PESTS

Slugs, stem rot, root rot, rust and leaf spot are possible problems.

Bleeding Heart
Dicentra

Height: 30–120 cm (12–47") **Spread:** 45–90 cm (18–36")
Flower colour: pink, white, red, purple **Blooms:** spring, summer
Hardiness: hardy

Room should be made in every garden for a bleeding heart. Tucked away in a shady spot, these lovely plants appear in spring, filling the garden with fresh promise. Now with the availability of the *formosa* types that can flower on and off all summer, the uses of bleeding hearts in the garden have been expanded.

PLANTING
Seeding: Start freshly ripened seed in a cold frame. Plants self-seed in the garden.
Planting out: Spring.
Spacing: 45–90 cm (18–36") apart.

GROWING

Bleeding hearts prefer **light shade** but tolerate full sun or full shade. Soil should be **moist** and **humus rich**. Though these plants prefer to remain evenly moist, they are quite drought tolerant, particularly if the weather doesn't get hot. Very dry summer conditions will cause the plant to die back, but it will revive in fall or the following spring.

It is most important for bleeding hearts to remain moist while in flower in order to prolong the flowering period. Constant summer moisture will keep the flowers coming until mid-summer. Common Bleeding Heart and Fringed Bleeding Heart rarely need dividing. Western Bleeding Heart can be divided every three years or so.

D. spectabilis

D. spectabilis 'Alba'

D. spectabilis

D. formosa

TIPS

Bleeding hearts can be naturalized in a woodland garden or grown in a border or rock garden. They make excellent early-season specimen plants. They do well near a pond or stream.

RECOMMENDED

D. 'Adrian Bloom' forms a compact clump of dark grey-green foliage. It grows about 30 cm (12") tall and spreads about 45 cm (18"). Bright red flowers are produced in late spring but continue to appear intermittently all summer.

D. exima (Fringed Bleeding Heart) forms a loose mounded clump of lacy, fern-like foliage. It grows 38–60 cm (15–24") tall and spreads about 45 cm (18"). The pink or white flowers are borne mostly in spring, but may be produced sporadically over summer. Hot, dry weather will cause the plant to go dormant during summer.

D. formosa (Western Bleeding Heart) is a low-growing, wide-spreading plant. It grows about 45 cm (18") tall and spreads 60–90 cm (24–36"). The pink flowers fade to white as they mature. This plant is likely to self-seed. **Var. *alba*** has white flowers. This is the most drought tolerant of the bleeding hearts and is most likely to continue flowering all summer. It can become invasive.

D. 'Luxuriant' is a low-growing hybrid with blue-green foliage and red-pink flowers. It grows about 30 cm (12") tall and spreads about 45 cm (18"). Flowers appear in spring and early summer.

D. spectabilis (Common Bleeding Heart) forms a large, elegant mound. It grows up to 120 cm (47") tall and spreads about 45 cm (18"). It bears late spring and early summer flowers. The inner petals are white while the outer petals are pink. This species is likely to die back in the summer heat and prefers light dappled shade. **'Alba'** has entirely white flowers.

D. 'Stuart Boothman' is a spreading perennial with blue-grey foliage. It grows about 30 cm (12") tall, with an equal or greater spread. Dark pink flowers are produced over a long period from spring to mid-summer.

PROBLEMS & PESTS
Slugs, downy mildew, *Verticillium* wilt, viruses, rust and fungal leaf spot can cause occasional problems.

These delicate plants are the perfect addition to the moist woodland garden. Plant them next to a shaded pond or stream.

D. exima

Butterfly Weed
Asclepias

Height: 45–90 cm (18–36") **Spread:** 30–60 cm (12–24")
Flower colour: orange, yellow, red
Blooms: mid-summer to fall **Hardiness:** hardy

Butterfly Weed is reputed to be one of the best plants for attracting butterflies to the garden. In Ontario the Monarch migration in fall is a wondrous event, so keep in mind the Monarch butterfly depends on Butterfly Weed for its food. The vivid orange flowers of *A. tuberosa* are good for cutting, and the seedpods colour nicely in fall.

PLANTING

Seeding: Fresh seed in cold frame in early spring.
Planting out: Spring.
Spacing: 30–60 cm (12–24") apart.

GROWING

Butterfly Weed prefers **full sun.** Any **well-drained soil** is tolerated, though a fertile soil is preferred. This plant is drought tolerant. Remove the plantlets that grow around the base of the plant for propagation. The deep tap root makes division very difficult.

TIPS

Use in meadow plantings, borders, on dry banks, in neglected areas and in wildflower, cottage and butterfly gardens.

These plants are slow to start in spring. Place a marker beside the plant in fall so you won't forget the plant is there and inadvertently dig it up in spring.

This plant is native to eastern North America. It is a major food source for the Monarch butterfly and will attract butterflies to your garden.

RECOMMENDED

A. tuberosa forms a clump of upright, leafy stems. It grows 45–90 cm (18–36") tall and spreads 30–60 cm (12–24"). It bears clusters of orange flowers. **'Gay Butterflies'** bears orange, yellow or red flowers.

PROBLEMS & PESTS

Aphids and mealybugs can be a problem on rare occasions.

Candytuft
Iberis

Height: 15–30 cm (6–12") **Spread:** 25–90 cm (10–36")
Flower colour: white **Blooms:** long period in spring
Hardiness: semi-hardy

*T*he rock gardens around older houses are often carpeted with Candytuft. A reminder of gardeners long gone, Candytuft returns each year and is a dependable sign of spring. The carpet of white blooms seems to have been created as the perfect backdrop for every colour and type of spring bulb from red tulips and yellow daffodils to purple Grape Hyacinths.

PLANTING
Seeding: Direct sow in spring.
Planting out: Spring.
Spacing: 15–30 cm (6–12") apart.

GROWING

Candytuft prefers **full sun**. Soil should be of **poor to average fertility, moist, well drained** and **neutral to alkaline.** Candytuft should be sheared back by about one-third once it has finished flowering to promote new, compact growth. Every two or three years it should be sheared back by one-half to two-thirds to discourage the development of too much woody growth and to encourage abundant flowering.

As the stems spread outwards, they may root where they touch the ground. These rooted ends may be cut away from the central plant. In spring, cut away any brown sections resulting from winter damage. Division is rarely required.

TIPS

Use Candytuft as an edging plant, in borders and rock gardens, along path edges, in the crevices of rock walls and with spring-blooming bulbs.

RECOMMENDED

I. sempervirens is a spreading, evergreen plant. It grows 15–30 cm (6–12") tall and spreads 40–90 cm (16–36"). It bears clusters of tiny, white flowers. **'Autumn Snow'** bears white flowers in spring and fall. **'Little Gem'** is a compact, spring-flowering plant that spreads only 25 cm (10"). **'Snowflake'** is a mounding plant that bears large white flowers.

PROBLEMS & PESTS

Occasional problems with slugs, caterpillars, damping off, grey mould and fungal leaf spot are possible.

If you are arriving home after dusk on a spring night, Candytuft will glow in the moonlight to welcome you.

122

Cardinal Flower
Lobelia

Height: 60–120 cm (24–48") **Spread:** 30–60 cm (12–24")
Flower colour: red, pink, white, yellow, blue **Blooms:** summer to fall
Hardiness: hardy to semi-hardy

It's a surprise to learn for the first time that our native cardinal flowers are related to the trailing *Lobelia* plant of hanging basket fame, but an even greater surprise to learn that they are both related to the bellflowers. Cardinal flower plants bear pure, charming, scarlet flowers and are a real asset in moist soil near ponds and in bog gardens—these plants like to get their feet wet.

PLANTING

Seeding: Direct sow in garden or cold frame in spring. Soil temperature at about 21° C (70° F).
Planting out: Spring.
Spacing: 30–45 cm (12–18") apart.

GROWING

Cardinal flowers prefer **full sun** and tolerate light shade or partial shade. Soil should be **fertile, slightly acidic** and **moist**. The soil should never be allowed to dry out for extended periods. Cardinal flowers are likely to self-seed quite easily. Because these plants are short-lived, lasting about four or five years, self-seeding is an easy way to ensure continuing generations of plants.

If you remove the spent flower spikes, be sure to allow at least a few of them to remain to spread their seeds. Don't worry too much, though—the lower flowers on a spike are likely to set seed before the top flowers are finished opening. Provide a mulch over the winter to protect the plants. Pinch plants in early summer to produce compact growth. Deadheading may encourage a second set of blooms. To divide, lift the entire plant and remove the new rosettes growing at the plant base in fall. Replant immediately in the garden.

L. cardinalis

L. cardinalis

L. cardinalis

L. siphilitica

TIPS

Cardinal flowers are best used in streamside or pondside plantings or in bog gardens.

Cardinal flowers may require a more acidic soil than other plants growing along a pond. If this is the case, they may be planted in a container of acidic soil and sunk into the ground at the edge of the pond.

RECOMMENDED

L. cardinalis (Cardinal Flower) forms an erect clump of bronze-green leaves. It grows 60–120 cm (24–48") tall and spreads 30–60 cm (12–24"). It bears spikes of bright red flowers from summer to fall. **'Alba'** has white flowers. **'Twilight Zone'** has light pink flowers

L. **'La Fresco'** bears jewel-toned, plum-purple flowers.

L. '**Queen Victoria**' forms a clump of reddish stems with maroon foliage and scarlet flowers. It grows about 90 cm (36") tall and spreads 30 cm (12").

L. siphilitica (Blue Cardinal Flower) forms an erect clump with bright green foliage. It grows 60–120 cm (24–48") tall and spreads 30–45 cm (12–18"). It bears spikes of blue flowers from mid-summer to fall. **Var. *alba*** has white flowers.

L. **x *speciosa*** (Hybrid Cardinal Flower) is the hardiest, strongest, most vigorous of the cardinal flowers. '**Complement**' has dark green foliage and bears red or blue-purple flowers.

L. '**Wildwood Splendor**' is a vigorous plant bearing deep purple flowers.

PROBLEMS & PESTS

Rare problems with slugs, rust, smut and leaf spot can occur.

Lobelia *was named after the Flemish botanist Mathias de l'Obel (1538–1616).*

L. 'Queen Victoria'

L. cardinalis

Catmint

Nepeta

Height: 30–90 cm (12–36") **Spread:** 45–90 cm (18–36")
Flower colour: blue, purple, white, pink
Blooms: spring and summer, sometimes again in fall
Hardiness: hardy to semi-hardy

*I*magine a catmint in a beautiful terra cotta pot outside a lovely wooden front door, the rich blue-purple flowers draping over the container's edge. This very image in a photograph was my introduction to this perennial. I've grown it ever since. It's a first-rate plant for blending with other perennials in the garden, offering a wide range of blues and purples. The taller varieties can even be used for cut flowers.

PLANTING

Seeding: Most popular hybrids and cultivars are sterile and cannot be grown from seed.
Planting out: Spring.
Spacing: 45–60 cm (18–24") apart.

GROWING

Catmint plants grow well in **full sun** or **partial shade**. Soil should be of **average fertility** and **well drained**. Plants will tend to flop over in rich soil. Pinch tips in June to delay flowering and make the plants more compact. Once the plants are almost finished blooming, you may cut them back by one-third to one-half. This will encourage new growth and might prompt them to bloom again in late summer or fall. Divide in spring or fall when the growth begins to look overgrown and dense.

N. x faassenii

Catmint has long been cultivated for its reputed medicinal and culinary qualities.

N. 'Six Hills Giant'

It is no mystery where this plant gets its name—cats love it! Dried leaves stuffed into cloth toys will amuse kittens for hours.

TIPS

Catmint plants can be used to edge borders and pathways and can be combined successfully in herb gardens and with roses in cottage gardens.

Take care if you decide to grow *N. cataria* (Catnip) because many cats are extremely attracted to this plant. You will be laying out a welcome mat for the neighbourhood cats to come and enjoy your garden. If you don't want cats in your garden, think twice before including this species in your plans. Cats do like the other catmints, but not to the same extent.

N. 'Blue Beauty'

RECOMMENDED

***N.* 'Blue Beauty'** ('Souvenir d'André Chaudron') forms an upright, spreading clump. It grows 45–90 cm (18–36") tall and spreads about 45 cm (18"). The grey-green foliage is fragrant and the large flowers are dark purple-blue.

N.* x *faassenii forms a clump of upright and spreading stems. It grows 45–90 cm (18–36") tall, with an equal spread. It bears spikes of blue or purple flowers. This hybrid and its cultivars are sterile and cannot be grown from seed. **'Dawn to Dusk'** has pink flowers. **'Dropmore'** has grey-green foliage and light purple flowers. **'Snowflake'** is low growing, compact and spreading with white flowers. It grows 30–60 cm (12–24") tall and spreads about 45 cm (18").

***N.* 'Six Hills Giant'** is a large, vigorous plant. It grows 90 cm (36") tall, or taller, and spreads 60 cm (24"). It bears large spikes of lavender blue flowers.

PROBLEMS & PESTS

Pest free, except for an occasional cat or bout of leaf spot.

Christmas Rose
Hellebore
Helleborus

Height: 30–45 cm (12–18") **Spread:** 30–45 cm (12–18")
Flower colour: white, green, pink, purple, yellow
Blooms: late winter to mid-spring **Hardiness:** semi-hardy

With their subtle flower colours and delicate appearance, Christmas roses are plants for true perennial connoisseurs. Terms like 'apple green,' 'russet,' 'maroon' and 'mulled wine' describe some of the shades found in these early-blooming harbingers of spring. Plant them near the house or along a path where their early arrival will cheer even the most downtrodden soul.

PLANTING

Seeding: Not recommended; seed is very slow to germinate.
Planting out: Spring or late summer.
Spacing: 30–45 cm (12–18") apart.

GROWING

Christmas roses prefer **light, dappled shade** in a sheltered site. Soil should be **fertile, moist, humus rich, neutral to alkaline** and **well drained**. These plants may self-seed. Protect plants with a mulch in winter, though in a mild winter you may find these perennials blooming through the snow in February. Divide in spring, after flowering, or whenever plants are becoming too crowded.

H. niger

H. orientalis

TIPS

Use these plants in a sheltered border or rock garden or naturalize in a woodland garden.

RECOMMENDED

H. niger (Christmas Rose) is a clump-forming evergreen. It grows 30 cm (12") tall and spreads 45 cm (18") and bears white or pink-flushed flowers in early spring.

H. orientalis (Lenten Rose) is a clump-forming evergreen perennial. It grows 30–45 cm (12–18") tall, with an equal spread. It bears, in mid-spring, white or greenish flowers that fade to pink.

ALTERNATE SPECIES

H. x hybridus plants are very attractive, with a wide range of flower colours, but are not as hardy as the previously mentioned species and will probably thrive in only the warmest parts of southern Ontario. The flowers can be white, purple, yellow, green or pink. The plants may be deciduous or evergreen.

PROBLEMS & PESTS

Problems may be caused by slugs, aphids, crown rot, leaf spot or black rot.

Columbine
Aquilegia

Height: 45–90 cm (18–36") **Spread:** 30–60 cm (12–24")
Flower colour: red, yellow, pink, purple, blue, white; colour of spurs
often differs from that of the petals
Blooms: spring, summer **Hardiness:** hardy

*T*he delicate and beautiful columbines add a touch of simple elegance to any garden. Blooming from the cool of spring through to mid-summer, these long-lasting flowers herald the passing of spring and the arrival of warm summer weather. Choose from tall, short, double, single, spurred or spurless and add the aura of an enchanted woodland clearing, even in an undeveloped suburban garden.

PLANTING

Seeding: Direct sow in spring.
Planting out: Spring.
Spacing: About 45 cm (18") apart.

GROWING

Columbines grow well in **full sun** or **partial shade**. Soil should be **fertile, moist** and **well drained**. Columbines adapt well to most soil conditions. These plants self-seed, and young seedlings can be transplanted. Division is not required but can be done to propagate desirable plants. They may take a while to recover as they dislike having their roots disturbed.

TIPS

Use columbines in a rock garden, a formal or casual border, or in a naturalized or woodland garden.

Columbines self-seed but are in no way invasive. Each year a few new plants may turn up near the parent plant. If you have a variety of columbines

Columbines are short-lived perennials that seed freely throughout the garden, and establish themselves in unexpected, and often charming, locations. If you wish to keep a particular form, you must preserve it carefully through frequent division or root cuttings.

planted near each other you may even wind up with a new cultivar. Columbines cross-breed easily, resulting in many hybrid forms. The wide variety of flower colours is the most interesting result. The new seedlings may not be identical to the parents and there is some likelihood that they will revert to the original species.

RECOMMENDED

A. canadensis (Wild Columbine, Canada Columbine) is native to most of eastern North America and is common in woodlands and fields in Ontario. It grows up to 60 cm (24") tall and spreads about 30 cm (12"). Yellow flowers with red spurs are borne in spring and summer.

A. vulgaris

A. x *hybrida* (*A.* x *cultorum*) (Hybrid Columbine) forms mounds of delicate foliage. Many groups of hybrids have been developed for their showy flowers of varied colours. When the exact parentage of a plant is uncertain, it is grouped under this heading. **'Double Pleat'** (Double Pleat Hybrids) grow 75–80 cm (30–32") tall. They bear double flowers in combinations of blue and white or pink and white. **'McKana Giants'** (McKana Hybrids) are popular and bear flowers in yellow, pink, red, purple, mauve and white. They grow up to 90 cm (36") tall. **'Dragonfly'** (Dragonfly Hybrids) have a wide range of flower colours on compact plants that grow up to 60 cm (24") tall and spread 30 cm (12").

A. vulgaris (European or Common Columbine) grows about 90 cm (36") tall and spreads 45 cm (18"). Flowers come in a wide variety of colours, and this species has been used to develop many hybrids and cultivars. **'Nora Barlow'** is a popular cultivar with double flowers in white, pink and green-tinged red.

PROBLEMS & PESTS

Mildew and rust can be troublesome during dry weather. Other problems can be caused by fungal leaf spot, aphids, caterpillars and leaf miners.

A. vulgaris

Coneflower
Echinacea
Echinacea

Height: 60–150 cm (24–60") **Spread:** 30–60 cm (12–24")
Flower colour: purple, pink, white; with rusty-orange centres
Blooms: summer **Hardiness:** hardy

Coneflower is also known as Echinacea, a popular herbal remedy. In the garden the Coneflower has impeccable credentials. It is a visual delight in all stages of flowering. From the time the barely pink-tinged petals start to unfold, to its full purple glory, Coneflower holds our attention. The large, dome-shaped central cone is beautiful at its peak and attractive as it dries and then is covered with snow in the winter garden. In our garden it was, sadly, a favourite feast for groundhogs.

PLANTING
Seeding: Direct sow in spring.
Planting out: Spring.
Spacing: 45 cm (18") apart.

GROWING
Coneflower grows well in **full sun** or **very light shade**. Any **well-drained soil** is tolerated, though an average or rich soil is preferred. The thick tap-root makes this plant drought resistant, but it prefers to have regular water. Deadheading early in the season is recommended as it prolongs the flowering season. Later in the season you may wish to leave the flowerheads in place.

The plants may self-seed, providing more plants. If you don't want them to self-seed, then remove all the flowerheads as they fade. Pinch plants back in early summer to encourage bushy growth that is less prone to mildew. Divide every four years or so in spring or fall.

'White Lustre'

'White Lustre'

TIPS

Use Coneflower in meadow gardens, informal borders, in groups or as single plants.

The dry flowerheads make an interesting feature in fall and winter gardens.

RECOMMENDED

E. purpurea is an upright plant with prickly hairs all over. It grows up to 150 cm (60") tall and spreads 45 cm (18"). The cultivars are generally about half this height. Purple flowers with orangy centres are borne from mid-summer to fall. **'Magnus'** bears large purple flowers, up to 18 cm (7") across, with orange centres. **'White Lustre'** bears white flowers with orange centres. **'White Swan'** is a compact plant with white flowers.

PROBLEMS & PESTS

Powdery mildew is the biggest problem. Also possible are leaf miners, bacterial spot and grey mould. Vine weevils may attack the roots.

Echinacea was discovered by the native peoples and was one of their most important medicines. It is a popular immunity booster in herbal medicine today.

Coral Bells
Alum Root
Heuchera

Height: 30–120 cm (12–48") **Spread:** 30–45 cm (12–18")
Flower colour: red, pink, white, yellow, purple
Blooms: spring, summer **Hardiness:** hardy

*T*he increasing popularity of coral bells is evident in the incredible amount of shelf space varieties get in nurseries today. One nursery alone listed over 40 cultivars in its latest catalogue! These plants, along with hostas, lungworts and foamflowers, helped start a trend toward using exciting foliage in the garden. The leaves of different species of coral bells can be purple, bronze, pewter, chocolate, veined or velvety, and the choices go on. Now improvements are being made to the flowers, so that this perennial truly has a one-two punch.

PLANTING
Seeding: Species, but not cultivars, may be started from seed in spring in cold frame.
Planting out: Spring.
Spacing: 30–45 cm (12–18") apart.

GROWING

Coral bells will grow best in **light or partial shade**. Foliage colours can bleach out in full sun and plants become leggy in full shade. Soil should be of **average to rich fertility, humus rich, neutral to alkaline, moist** and **well drained**. Good air circulation is essential. If the soil is acidic, then horticultural lime should be applied to the soil each year.

The spent flowers should be removed to prolong the blooming period. Every two or three years coral bells should be dug up to remove the oldest, woodiest roots and stems. Coral bells may be divided at this time, if desired, then replanted with the crown just above soil level. Cultivars may be propagated by division in spring or fall.

TIPS

Use coral bells as edging plants, clustered in woodland gardens or as groundcovers in low traffic areas. Combine different foliage types for an interesting display.

Coral bells have a strange habit of pushing themselves up out of the soil—mulch in fall if the plants begin heaving from the ground.

H. sanguinea

Cut flowers can be used in arrangements.

'Firefly'

'Palace Purple'

These delicate woodland plants will enhance your garden with their bright colours, attractive foliage and airy sprays of flowers.

'Palace Purple'

RECOMMENDED

Most of the cultivars listed are hybrids developed from crosses between the various species. They are grouped with one of their acknowledged parents in the following list.

H. americana is a mound-forming plant. The heart-shaped foliage is marbled and veined in bronze when it is young and matures to deep green. The plant grows about 45 cm (18") tall and spreads 30 cm (12"). Cultivars have been developed for their attractive and variable foliage. **'Chocolate Veil'** has dark chocolatey-purple leaves with silvery patches between the veins. Its flowers are greenish purple. **'Pewter Veil'** has silvery-purple leaves with dark grey veining. Its flowers are white flushed with pink.

H. x brizioides is a group of mound-forming hybrids, developed through extensive cross-breeding of the various species for their attractive flowers. They grow 30–75 cm (12–30") tall and spread 30–45 cm (12–18"). **'Firefly'** has fragrant, bright pinkish-red flowers. **'June Bride'** has large, white flowers. **'Raspberry Regal'** is a larger plant, growing up to 120 cm (48") tall. The foliage is strongly marbled and the flowers are bright red.

H. micrantha is a mounding, clump-forming plant. It grows up to 90 cm (36") tall. The foliage is grey-green and the flowers are white. The species is not common in gardens, but there are many cultivars which are very common. **'Chocolate Ruffles'** has ruffled, glossy, brown foliage with purple undersides that give the leaves a bronzed appearance. **Var. *diversifolia* 'Palace Purple'** is one of the best known cultivars of all the Coral Bells. This compact cultivar has deep purple foliage and white blooms. It grows 45–50 cm (18–20") tall. This cultivar can be started from seed, but only some of the seedlings will be true to type. **'Pewter Moon'** has light pink flowers and silvery leaves with bronzy-purple veins. **'Bressingham Hybrids'** are compact hybrids that can be started from seed. Flowers will be pink or red.

H. sanguinea is the hardiest species. It forms a low-growing mat of foliage. It grows 30–45 cm (12–18") tall, with an equal spread. The dark green foliage is marbled with silver. The red, pink or white flowers are borne in summer. **'Coral Cloud'** has pinkish-red flowers and glossy, crinkled leaves. **'Frosty'** has red flowers and silver-variegated foliage. **'Northern Fire'** has red flowers and leaves mottled with silver.

PROBLEMS & PESTS

Healthy coral bells have very few problems. In stressed situations, they can be afflicted with foliar nematodes, powdery mildew, rust or leaf spot.

'Palace Purple'

'Pewter Veil'

Coreopsis
Tickseed
Coreopsis

Height: 30–80 cm (12–36") **Spread:** 30–60 cm (12–24")
Flower colour: yellow, pink or orange
Blooms: early to late summer **Hardiness:** hardy to semi-hardy

Three cheers for these native North American plants. Coreopsis fill the garden with their sunny dispositions. I particularly like *Coreopsis verticillata* 'Golden Showers.' It blooms for two solid months, and if you deadhead or shear it back, you'll get some late-season flowering as well. I welcome those yellow daisy shapes when the purple asters are coming on.

Gardeners have had a love affair for the past few years with the cultivar 'Moonbeam,' which has intriguing pale yellow flowers. It is a lovely plant but not as vigorous as 'Golden Showers.'

PLANTING

Seeding: Plant seeds directly in spring. Seeds may be sown indoors in winter, but soil must be kept fairly cool, at 13–16° C (55–61° F), in order to germinate.

Planting out: Spring.

Spacing: 30–45 cm (12–18") apart.

GROWING

Grow coreopsis in **full sun**. Soil should be **average, sandy** and **well drained**. Coreopsis plants will die in moist, cool locations. Overly fertile soil causes long, floppy growth. Daily deadheading will keep plants in constant summer bloom. Use scissors to snip out tall stems. Frequent division may be required to keep plants vigorous.

C. verticillata

TIPS

Coreopsis plants are versatile—they are useful in formal and informal borders and in a meadow planting or cottage garden. These plants look nice individually or in large groups.

Shear plants by one-half in late spring for more compact growth.

Mass plant coreopsis to fill in a dry, exposed bank where nothing else will grow, and you will enjoy the bright, sunny flowers all summer long.

C. verticillata

If plants blacken from frost, remove the blackened foliage in fall to prevent slugs from using it as a nursery.

RECOMMENDED

C. auriculata (Mouse-Eared Tickseed) is low growing and well suited to rock gardens or fronts of borders. It grows 30–60 cm (12–24") tall and will continue to creep outwards without becoming invasive.

C. rosea (Pink Tickseed) is an unusual species with pink flowers. It grows 60 cm (24") tall and 30 cm (12") wide. This species is more shade and water tolerant than the other species.

C. verticillata (Thread-Leaf Coreopsis) is a mound-forming plant with attractive, finely divided foliage. It grows 60–80 cm (24–32") tall and

C. rosea

45 cm (18") wide. It is a long-lived species and will need dividing less frequently than most species. Divide it if some of the plant seems to be dying out. **'Golden Showers'** has large, golden yellow flowers and ferny foliage. **'Moonbeam'** forms a compact mound of delicate foliage. The flowers are a light, creamy yellow.

PROBLEMS & PESTS

Occasional problems with slugs, bacterial spot, *Botrytis* blight, aster yellows, powdery mildew, downy mildew and fungal spot are possible.

C. verticillata

'Moonbeam'

Self seeds??

Corydalis
Corydalis

Height: 20–45 cm (8–18") **Spread:** 20–30 cm (8–12")
Flower colour: blue, yellow **Blooms:** spring, summer
Hardiness: semi-tender to tender

Stylish gardeners fuss over *Corydalis flexuosa* with its breathtaking blue flowers, but I still enjoy *Corydalis lutea* for its ferny foliage, tubular yellow flowers and undemanding ways. In any light or any soil conditions Yellow Corydalis will thrive. In my garden it even popped up in a dusting of sand and debris at the base of a pile of bricks. Even a single planting will invariably self-seed and spread to the most unlikely places in the garden. This determined but shallow-rooted plant is easy to pull up and control if it begins to get out of hand. All types of corydalis will put on a wonderful spring show when combined with Sweet Woodruff, Canada Wild Ginger and Jacob's Ladder.

PLANTING

Seeding: Sow fresh seed in garden in early fall. Germination can be erratic.
Planting out: Spring.
Spacing: 30 cm (12") apart.

GROWING

Corydalis plants grow well in **full sun to light shade.** Soil should be of **average to rich fertility, humus rich** and **well drained.** Too much sun may scorch plants in summer. Cut out yellow foliage, and fresh growth will cover the plants in fall. This plant self-seeds and can be propagated by transplanting the tiny seedlings as they turn up. Division can be done in spring or early summer, but corydalis resent having their roots disturbed.

TIPS

Use corydalis in woodland or rock gardens, in borders and rock walls, to edge paths or naturalize in unused or under-used areas. Corydalis plants love to grow between rocks. They re-seed readily in gravel paths but seedlings are easy to pull and transplant.

RECOMMENDED

C. **'Blue Panda'** is a cultivar of uncertain parentage. This compact plant grows to 20 cm (8") in height. It bears bright, sky blue flowers in late spring and early summer. This plant is less invasive than the species are.

C. flexuosa (Blue Corydalis) is an erect plant with blue flowers. It grows 30 cm (12") tall and spreads 20 cm (8") or more. This plant prefers partial shade and may go dormant once it is finished flowering.

C. lutea (Yellow Corydalis) is a mound-forming perennial that bears yellow flowers from late spring to early fall. It grows 30–45 cm (12–18") tall and spreads 30 cm (12") or more. This is the hardiest species; it is also the most vigorous and can become invasive. It's invasive, self-seeding habit can be used to your advantage if you plant it in a tough spot where nothing else will grow.

PROBLEMS & PESTS

Rare problems with downy mildew and rust are possible.

Cupid's Dart
Catananche

Height: 45–90 cm (18–36") **Spread**: 30 cm (12")
Flower colour: blue, purple, white
Blooms: mid-summer to fall **Hardiness:** hardy

*T*he lavender-blue flowers of Cupid's Dart seem to have been created by the stroke of a watercolour painter's brush. The plant and foliage are rather nondescript, but when mixed with bushy foliage plants, the flowers of Cupid's Dart truly shine. Let it peek out through the soft, grey foliage of a 'Silver Mound' artemisia or combine it with the tall, ferny Annual Cosmos. Then the flowers can be fully enjoyed and you won't be asking yourself why you included an otherwise rather dull plant in your border.

PLANTING
Seeding: Direct sow in garden in mid- to late spring. Soil temperature at about 21° C (70° F).
Planting out: Spring.
Spacing: 30 cm (12") apart.

GROWING
Cupid's Dart prefers **full sun** but tolerates partial shade. Soil should be **sandy, humus rich** and **well drained**. Cupid's Dart dislikes wet soil. Find a spot where the ground is well drained and dries up quickly in spring. This fast-growing perennial will flower the first year from seed, and it can be grown as an annual. Divide every year or so to keep the plant vigorous.

TIPS
Use in borders, in mass plantings, on dry banks, and in cottage gardens, rock gardens and planters.

The cut flowers can be used in fresh and dried arrangements.

RECOMMENDED
C. caerulea is a clump-forming perennial with narrow grass-like foliage. It grows 45–90 cm (18–36") tall and spreads 30 cm (12"). Blue or purple-blue flowers are borne from mid-summer to frost. **'Bicolor'** has white flowers with purple centres.

PROBLEMS & PESTS
Powdery mildew can occur, but is unlikely to be serious.

Daylily
Hemerocallis

Height: 30–120 cm (12–48") **Spread:** 30–120 cm (12–48")
Flower colour: every colour except blue and pure white
Blooms: spring, summer **Hardiness:** hardy

Some devoted gardeners will stop at nothing to include the newest daylily in their gardens, perhaps spending a hundred dollars or more for the variety that no one else has yet obtained. The choices in colour, blooming period, size and texture combined with the adaptability and durability of this perennial make it easy to see why daylilies are so popular. To more deeply delve into the world of the daylily you can even join a society and perhaps learn to breed your own new cultivar. Then you may find you really do have a daylily that no one else has.

PLANTING

Seeding: Not recommended; hybrids and culti-vars don't come true to type from seed.
Planting out: Spring.
Spacing: 30–120 cm (12–48").

GROWING

Daylilies will grow in any light from **full sun** to **full shade**. The deeper the shade, the fewer flowers that will be produced. Soil should be **fertile, moist** and **well drained**, but these plants adapt to most condi-tions and are hard to kill once they are established. Deadhead small varieties to keep them blooming for as long as possible. Feed your daylilies in spring and mid-summer to produce the best display of blooms. Divide every two to three years to keep plants vigorous and to propagate them. They can be left indefinitely without dividing.

Taken from the Greek words for day 'hemera' and beauty 'kallos', the genus and the common name explain that these lovely blooms last only one day.

TIPS

Daylilies can be planted alone or grouped in borders, on banks and in ditches to control erosion. They can be naturalized in woodland or meadow gardens. Small varieties are nice in planters.

Be careful when deadheading purple-flowered daylilies, as they can stain fingers and clothes.

RECOMMENDED

There is an almost infinite number of forms, sizes and colours in a variety of species, cultivars and hybrids. See your local garden centre or daylily grower to find out what's available and most suitable for your garden.

PROBLEMS & PESTS

Generally these plants are pest free. Rare problems with rust, *Hemerocallis* gall midge, aphids, spider mites, thrips and slugs are possible.

Dead Nettle
Spotted Dead Nettle, Lamium
Lamium

Height: 20–60 cm (8–24") **Spread:** indefinite
Flower colour: white, pink, yellow, mauve
Blooms: spring, summer **Hardiness:** hardy to semi-hardy

*T*hose shade-loving folks who have trouble gardening under their beloved maple trees can turn to dead nettles for salvation. These attractive plants, with their striped, dotted, or banded silver and green foliage, hug the ground and thrive when provided with the barest necessities of life. Their adaptability means dead nettles can be invasive and will overwhelm more timid plants without a second thought. For this reason they are best grown in the difficult spots where those timid plants fear to tread.

PLANTING
Seeding: Not recommended; cultivars don't come true to type.
Planting out: Spring.
Spacing: 30–60 cm (12–24") apart.

GROWING
Dead nettles prefer **partial to light shade** and tolerate full sun but can get leggy in it. Soil should be of **average fertility, humus rich, moist** and **well drained**. The more fertile the soil the more vigorously the plants will grow. If the plant is becoming invasive, pull some of it up, making sure to remove the fleshy roots.

These plants are drought tolerant when grown in the shade but can develop bare patches if the soil is allowed to dry out frequently for extended periods. Divide and replant if bare spots become unsightly. Divide in fall when bare patches develop.

L. galeobdolon 'Variegatum'

L. maculatum

This plant is commonly known as dead nettle because its leaves look like those of stinging nettle.

TIPS

Dead nettles can be useful groundcovers for woodland or shade gardens or under shrubs in a border where this plant can keep the weeds down. Keep in mind that dead nettles can be quite invasive and are likely to overwhelm less vigorous plants.

Dead nettles will remain more compact if sheared back after flowering.

RECOMMENDED

L. maculatum is a low-growing, spreading perennial. It grows 20 cm (8") tall and spreads at least 90 cm (36"). The green leaves often have white or silvery markings. White, pink or mauve flowers are borne in summer. **'Aureum'** has gold or yellow foliage with white striped centres. Its flowers

'Florentinum'

'Florentinum'

are pink. **'Beacon Silver'** has green-edged, silver foliage. The flowers are pink. **'Chequers'** has green leaves with silver stripes down the centres. The flowers are mauve. **'White Nancy'** has white flowers and silver leaves with green margins.

ALTERNATE SPECIES

L. galeobdolon (White Archangel) can be quite invasive, though the cultivars are less so. It grows 30–60 cm (12–24") tall and spreads indefinitely. The flowers are yellow. **'Florentinum'** ('Variegatum') has silver foliage with green margins. **'Silver Angel'** is a prostrate cultivar with silvery foliage.

PROBLEMS & PESTS

Rare problems with slugs, powdery mildew, downy mildew and leaf spot are possible.

'Beacon Silver'

Delphinium
Candle Delphinium, Candle Larkspur
Delphinium

Height: 90–180 cm (36–72") **Spread:** 60–90 cm (24–36")
Flower colour: blue, purple, pink, white or bicolours
Blooms: late spring, early summer
Hardiness: hardy

Delphiniums are the royalty of the English perennial border. In that mild climate with abundant moisture, tall, stately delphiniums command attention at the back of the border. In the hot and humid summers of Ontario, delphiniums never seem to do quite as well. Nonetheless, bold gardeners venture on, nurturing these beautiful plants, because even if delphiniums in Ontario never achieve the magnificence they are capable of, they are still among the most beautiful perennials for a dramatic, back-of-the-border display.

PLANTING

Seeding: Seeds started directly in the garden in spring will produce flowers the following year. Seedlings may not be true to type.

Planting out: Spring or fall. Plant with crown at soil level to avoid crown rot.

Spacing: 60 cm (24") apart.

GROWING

Grow in a **full sun** location that is well protected from strong winds. Soil should be **fertile, moist** and **humus rich** with **excellent drainage**. Delphiniums love manure mixed into the soil.

D. grandiflorum

D. x elatum

D. x belladonna

Delphis *is the Greek word for dolphin, which lends itself well to this flower: the petals of the flowers resemble the nose and fins of a dolphin.*

D. x elatum

To encourage a second flush of smaller blooms, remove the first flower spikes once they begin to fade and before they begin to set seed. Cut them off just above the foliage. New shoots will begin to grow and the old foliage will fade back. The old growth may then be cut right back allowing new growth to fill in. These heavy feeders require fertilizer twice a year, in spring and summer. Delphiniums require division each year, in spring, to keep them vigorous.

TIPS

Delphiniums are classic cottage garden plants. Their height and need for staking relegate them to the back of the border where they make a magnificent blue-toned backdrop for warmer foreground flowers such as peonies, poppies and black-eyed Susans.

The tall flower spikes have hollow centres and are easily broken if exposed to the wind. Each flower spike will need to be individually staked. Stakes should be installed as soon as the flower spike reaches 30 cm (12") in height. You could use a wire tomato cage for a clump.

RECOMMENDED

D. x belladonna (Belladonna Hybrids) bears flowers of blue, white or mauve in loose, branched spikes. It grows 90–120 cm (36–48") tall and spreads 30–45 cm (12–18"). **'Blue Bees'** has pale blue flowers with white centres. **'Wendy'** has dark purple-blue flowers.

D. x elatum (Elatum Hybrids) bears densely held flowers of blue, purple, white, pink or yellow on tall spikes. They are divided into three height categories. Dwarfs grow up to 1.5 m (5'), mediums grow 1.7 m (5 1/2'), talls grow 2 m (6'), and all spread up to 90 cm (36"). **'Blue Dawn'** has blue flowers with dark blue centres. **'Turkish Delight'** has pink flowers with white centres.

D. grandiflorum (*D. chinense*) bears flowers of blue, purple or white in loose, branched clusters. It grows 20–50 cm (8–20") tall and spreads up to 30 cm (12"). **'Album'** has white flowers. **'Blue Butterfly'** bears bright blue flowers on compact plants.

PROBLEMS & PESTS

Problems can be caused by slugs, powdery mildew, bacterial and fungal leaf spot, grey mould, crown and root rot, white rot, rust, white smut, leaf smut and damping off. While this is a daunting list, remember that healthy plants are less susceptible to problems.

D. grandiflorum

These are plants so gorgeous in bloom that you can build a garden or plan a party around their flowering.

Doronicum
Leopard's Bane
Doronicum

Height: 30–75 cm (12–30") **Spread:** 30–90 cm (12–36")
Flower colour: yellow **Blooms:** mid-spring to early summer
Hardiness: hardy to semi-hardy

By September many gardeners are tired of daisy-like flowers, but in spring the bright, sunny, simple flowers of Doronicum are welcome and uplifting. Often overlooked because it falls dormant and completely disappears from the garden in summer, this moisture-loving perennial is perfect for damp spots in the garden. Doronicum looks great with tulips and forget-me-nots in spring, but be sure to plant some other moisture-loving, bushy perennials like meadowsweet or astilbe to fill in the empty space and remind you to water once summer rolls around.

PLANTING

Seeding: Sow seed on soil surface in spring; keep soil temperature at about 21° C (70° F).
Planting out: Spring or fall.
Spacing: 30–60 cm (12–24") apart.

GROWING

Doronicum grows well in **full sun, partial shade** or **light shade**. Soil should be of **average to high fertility, moist, humus rich** and **sandy**. These plants do not tolerate drought, but don't like to stand in water. Doronicum becomes dormant in summer. Allow other plants to fill the space Doronicum leaves in summer, but don't forget it is there and don't allow the soil to completely dry out. Divide every two or three years in spring or late summer.

TIPS

Use in a border, cottage garden or naturalized garden.

Annuals planted near Doronicum will fill in, over the summer, the space left by the dormant plant. Take care not to disturb the roots of the Doronicum while planting annuals.

RECOMMENDED

D. orientale (*D. caucasicum*) is a shallow-rooted, spreading, mounding plant. It grows 30–60 cm (12–24") tall and spreads 30–90 cm (12–36"). Yellow daisy-like flowers are borne in abundance in spring. **'Little Leo'** is a compact cultivar with semi-double yellow flowers. **'Magnificum'** is a large plant with large flowers. It can grow up to 75 cm (30") tall.

D. **'Miss Mason'** is a hybrid whose foliage is more persistent over the summer.

PROBLEMS & PESTS

Powdery mildew, aphids, leaf spot and root rot are uncommon, but possible, problems.

Your so lucky if you can grow this!

English Daisy

Bellis

Height: 5–20 cm (2–8") **Spread:** 5–20 cm (2–8")
Flower colour: yellow-centered, white, pink or red
Blooms: mid-spring to late summer **Hardiness:** semi-hardy

*I*n mild climates that never get too hot or too cold, these dainty and adorable little flowers can become a real nuisance. They turn up in lawns and flowerbeds all over the garden once planted. In the hot and humid summers of Ontario, English Daisy is much better behaved. Putting on a good show in spring, it fades into the backgound in summer only to revive with the cooler fall weather. The invasive tendencies are curbed and these plants can be enjoyed without gaining weed status in your neighbour's lawn. Plant lots of spring bulbs around them for a stunning spring display.

PLANTING

Seeding: Spring or summer for flowers the following spring.
Planting out: Spring.
Spacing: 5–20 cm (2–8") apart.

GROWING

English Daisy grows well in **full sun, partial shade** or **light shade**. Soil should be of **average to high fertility, cool, moist** and **humus rich**. A winter mulch will help protect English Daisy from the cold. Divide in mid-spring or late summer.

TIPS

Use English Daisy on rock walls, in open woodland gardens, in planters, to edge borders and as a groundcover.

'Pomponette'

English Daisy plants have the habit of self-seeding and may show up where you least expect them, including in your lawn. Deadheading to control spread is possible but decidedly time-consuming because English Daisy is low growing. Being a personal fan of flowering plants in lawns, I simply let these small and attractive flowers be. However, if immaculate lawns are required, then place this species in beds that are well away from lawns and consider taking the time to deadhead.

RECOMMENDED

B. perennis is a low, spreading perennial. White, pink or red flowers have yellow centres. Where it is not hardy it can be grown as an annual. **'Dresden China'** is a small, compact plant with light pink, double flowers. **'Habanero'** has pink, white or red flowers with long petals. **'Pomponette'** has pink, red or white flowers with quilled petals. The petals are rolled into tubes, lengthwise, giving the flowers a 'quilled' appearance. **'White Pearl'** has white, double flowers.

PROBLEMS & PESTS

Fungal leaf spot and aphids are possible, but not serious, problems.

Euphorbia
Spurge
Euphorbia

Height: 30–60 cm (12–24") **Spread:** 45–60 cm (18–24")
Flower colour: yellow, green **Blooms:** spring to mid-summer
Hardiness: hardy

This wide and varied group of plants includes the popular holiday poinsettia, plants that resemble cactus and several frost-hardy perennial garden plants. *E. polychroma* is an attractive, mounding plant with bright yellow bracts produced in spring and early summer when it flowers. It's a favorite at May 24 plant sales when it's often at its peak. Another type that's been gaining popularity is *E. dulcis* 'Chameleon' with burgundy and red foliage. Both euphorbias provide an excellent display of fall colour.

PLANTING

Seeding: Use fresh seed for best germination rates. Start seed in cold frame in spring.
Planting out: Spring or fall.
Spacing: 45 cm (18").

GROWING

Euphorbias grow well in **full sun** and **light shade**. Soil should be of **average fertility, moist, humus rich** and **well drained**. These plants are drought tolerant and can be invasive in too fertile a soil. Euphorbias can be propagated by stem cuttings and they may self-seed in the garden. Division is rarely required. Euphorbias dislike being disturbed once established.

TIPS

Use euphorbias in a mixed or herbaceous border, rock garden or lightly shaded woodland garden.

You may wish to wear gloves when handling this plant because some people find the milky sap irritates their skin.

If you are cutting the stems for propagation, dip the cut ends in hot water before planting to stop the sticky white sap from running.

RECOMMENDED

E. dulcis is a compact, upright plant. It grows about 30 cm (12") tall, with an equal spread. The dark bronze-green leaves turn red and orange in fall. **'Chameleon'** has purple-red foliage that turns darker purple in fall.

E. polychroma (*E. epithimoides*) is a mounding, clump-forming perennial.

It grows 30–60 cm (12–24") tall and spreads 45–60 cm (18–24"). The inconspicuous flowers are surrounded by long-lasting, yellow bracts. The foliage turns shades of purple, red or orange in fall. There are several cultivars, though the species is more commonly available. **'Candy'** has yellow bracts and flowers, but the leaves and stems are tinged with purple. **'Emerald Jade'** is a compact plant that grows to 35 cm (14") in height. The bracts are yellow, but the flowers are bright green.

PROBLEMS & PESTS

Aphids, spider mites and nematodes are possible, as well as fungal root rot in poorly drained, wet soil.

Evening Primrose
Oenothera

Height: 15–90 cm (6–36") **Spread:** 30–45 cm (12–18")
Flower colour: yellow, pink, white
Blooms: spring, summer **Hardiness:** hardy

*E*vening primroses have created quite a stir among advocates of herbal remedies, but for gardeners the plants remain beautiful perennials that are easy to care for. These North American natives were long considered weeds but have recently found a home with gardeners looking for low-maintenance plants. Evening primroses boost the confidence of beginning gardeners and are well loved for their abundant, simple, poppy-like flowers.

PLANTING
Seeding: Start in cold frame in mid-spring.
Planting out: Spring.
Spacing: About 30 cm (12") apart.

GROWING

Evening primroses prefer **full sun**. Soil should be of **poor to average fertility** and be **very well drained**. These plants self-seed easily and can become invasive in a very fertile soil. They aren't bothered by hot, humid weather. Divide in spring.

TIPS

Use these plants in the front of a border and to edge borders and pathways. Evening primroses will brighten a gravelly bank or rock garden.

Evening primroses can be a bit invasive, self-seeding in unexpected places in the garden.

RECOMMENDED

O. fremontii bears yellow flowers over a long season and the foliage forms a low mat. It grows 15 cm (6") high and spreads 30–45 cm (12–18"). **'Lemon Silver'** is a new Canadian introduction with silver-blue leaves and large lemon yellow flowers.

O. fruticosa (Sundrops, Evening Primrose) grows 45–90 cm (18–36") tall and spreads 30–45 cm (12–18"). It bears bright yellow flowers in summer. The foliage of this plant turns red after a light frost. **'Summer Solstice'** ('Sonnenwende') is a smaller, compact plant. It bears larger flowers for a long period from early summer to early fall. The foliage turns red in summer and burgundy in fall.

O. speciosa (Showy Evening Primrose) is a lanky, upright or spreading plant. It grows 15–60 cm (6–24") tall and spreads 30–45 cm (12–18"). Its flowers can be pink or white. **'Pinkie'** is a night-blooming plant with white flowers that mature to pink with darker pink veins.

PROBLEMS & PESTS

Rare problems with downy mildew, powdery mildew, leaf gall, rust and leaf spot are possible. Plants may develop root rot in poorly drained soil.

O. speciosa

Another common name for this plant is evening star, because at night the petals emit phosphorescent light.

O. fruticosa

False Dragonhead
Obedient Plant
Physostegia

Height: 30–120 cm (12–48") **Spread:** 30–60 cm (12–24")
Flower colour: pink, purple, white
Blooms: mid-summer to fall **Hardiness:** hardy

Though the individual flowers will stay where you put them, giving the plant one of its common names, the plant itself rarely stays put, self-seeding and turning up all over the garden. 'Variegata,' with its cream-margined green leaves and bright pink flowers, seems to be one of the least invasive. This cultivar is popular among gardeners who admire variegated plants.

PLANTING
Seeding: Sow in early fall or in spring. Soil temperature should be about 21–24° C (70–75° F). Protect fall-started seedlings from winter cold.
Planting out: Spring or fall.
Spacing: 30–60 cm (12–24") apart.

GROWING

False Dragonhead prefers **full sun** and tolerates partial or light shade. Soil should be of **average to high fertility** and **moist**. In a fertile soil this plant will be more vigorous and will possibly need staking. Choose a compact cultivar to avoid the need for staking. Plants can become invasive. Divide in early to mid-spring, once ground can be worked, every two years or so to curtail invasiveness.

TIPS

Use in borders, cottage gardens and informal and natural gardens. False Dragonhead can be cut for use in fresh arrangements.

The flowers can be bent around on the stems and will stay put where you leave them. It is this unusual habit that gives the plant the name 'Obedient Plant.'

RECOMMENDED

P. virginiana has a spreading root system from which upright stems sprout. It grows 60–120 cm (24–48")

tall and spreads 60 cm (24"), or more. **'Crown of Snow'** ('Snow Crown') has white flowers. **'Pink Bouquet'** bears bright pink flowers. **'Summer Snow'** is a more compact, less-invasive plant with white flowers. **'Variegata'** is a desirable variegated specimen with cream-margined leaves and bright pink flowers.

P. **'Vivid'** bears bright purple-pink flowers. This compact cultivar grows 30–60 cm (12–24") tall and spreads 30 cm (12").

PROBLEMS & PESTS

Rare problems with rust and slugs are possible.

False Rockcress
Rock Cress, Aubrieta
Aubrieta

Height: 5–15 cm (2–6") **Spread:** 60 cm (24")
Flower colour: white, pink, purple **Blooms:** spring, early summer
Hardiness: hardy to semi-hardy

This is one of the most popular and most beautiful of the low-growing, spring-flowering perennials. Though it flowers for only a short period in spring, the purple, pink or red flowers look fetching capping off rock walls, mounding in rock gardens or spilling out of planters. The show is so impressive that you are bound to forgive this plant for receding into the background in summer. 'Variegata' has yellow-margined leaves that provide some interest once the plant has finished flowering.

PLANTING

Seeding: Seeds from garden plants may not come true to type. Purchased seed is more dependable. Start seed in spring. Soil temperature should be about 21° C (70° F).

Planting out: Fall.

Spacing: 45 cm (18") apart.

GROWING

False Rockcress prefers **full sun,** but will tolerate partial shade. Soil should be of **average fertility** and **well drained with rocks or gravel** mixed in. This plant also prefers soil to be a little on the **alkaline** side.

False Rockcress should be sheared back by half once it has finished flowering. This will encourage compact growth and may occasionally result in a second flush of flowers later in the season. Every year or two, in fall, False Rockcress will need dividing in order to prevent the clump from thinning and dying out in the middle. Shear the old flowers because seedlings will not bloom true to type.

False Rockcress is popular in England, where cascades of purple flowers slip over rock walls and brighten rainy spring days.

TIPS

Use False Rockcress in the crevices of a rock wall, between the paving stones of a pathway, in a rock garden, along the edge of a border or beneath taller plants.

RECOMMENDED

There are many cultivars, and their parentage is somewhat uncertain. Depending on the source they can be attributed to ***A. deltoidea*** or ***A. x cultorum***. All are low, mounding or cascading perennials that flower in early or mid-spring. **'Purple Cascade'** bears purple flowers and is commonly available. **'Red Carpet'** bears rose red flowers. **'Variegata'** bears blue-purple flowers and has gold-variegated foliage. **'Whitewell Gem'** has purple flowers.

PROBLEMS & PESTS

Rare problems with aphids, nematodes or flea beetles can occur.

This low-grower can spread quite far but is rarely invasive in the garden.

False Solomon's Seal

Smilacina

Height: 90 cm (36") **Spread:** 60–120 cm (24–48")
Flower colour: white **Blooms:** mid- to late spring
Hardiness: hardy

F alse Solomon's Seal is a charming, native, woodland perennial. It is similar to Solomon's Seal (*Polygonatum*), but instead of having small bell-like flowers dangling from beneath the stems, it bears large plumes of flowers at the ends of the stems. Adding to the attractive features are the bright red berries that ripen in late summer. This is an ideal plant to include in a damp woodland garden.

PLANTING

Seeding: Not recommended.
Planting out: Spring or fall.
Spacing: 60 cm (24") apart.

GROWING

False Solomon's Seal grows well in **light or full shade**. Soil should be of **average fertility, humus rich, acidic, moist** and **well drained**. Add peat moss to the soil when planting to provide the acidic, humus-rich conditions this plant enjoys. Divide in spring.

TIPS

Use in an open woodland or natural garden. In a shaded border it can be combined with hostas and other shade-loving perennials.

RECOMMENDED

S. racemosa (*Maianthemum racemosum*) forms a spreading clump of upright, arching stems. White plume-like flowers in spring are followed by berries that ripen in late summer and fall.

PROBLEMS & PESTS

Rust and leaf spot are possible but rarely serious.

The berries of this plant ripen in an unusual way. The unripe green berries develop little red spots that eventually cover the entire fruit.

Foamflower
Tiarella

Height: 10–30 cm (4–12") **Spread:** 30–60 cm (12–24")
Flower colour: white, pink **Blooms:** spring, sometimes to early summer
Hardiness: hardy

*T*here is much to praise in the lovely foamflowers. They form handsome groundcovers in shaded areas, with attractive leaves and delicate, starry, white flowers. In a mass planting the flowers look like fireflies dancing over the ground. Hybridizers are working to enhance this perennial even more. 'Oakleaf' is an outstanding selection with lobed foliage and red winter colour. Foamflowers combine gracefully with ferns.

PLANTING
Seeding: Start in cold frame in spring.
Planting out: Spring.
Spacing: 15–60 cm (6–24") apart.

GROWING
Foamflowers prefer **partial, light or full shade** avoiding afternoon sun. Soil should be **humus rich, moist** and **slightly acidic**. These plants adapt to most soils. Deadheading will encourage re-blooming. Divide in spring.

TIPS
Foamflowers are excellent groundcovers for shaded and woodland gardens. They can be included in shaded borders and left to naturalize in wild gardens.

If foliage fades or rusts in summer, cut it partway to the ground and fresh new growth will emerge.

Foamflowers spread by underground stolons, which are easily pulled up to stop the plant from spreading too far.

RECOMMENDED
T. cordifolia is a low-growing, spreading perennial. This plant is attractive enough to be grown for the foliage alone, and cultivars with interesting variegation are starting to become available. Spikes of foamy flowers are borne in spring. This plant is a native of eastern North America.

T. **'Maple Leaf'** is a clump-forming hybrid with bronzy-green, maple-like leaves and pink-flushed flowers.

T. wherryi is similar to *T. cordifolia,* but it forms a clump and bears more flowers. **'Oakleaf'** forms a dense clump of dark green leaves and bears pink flowers.

PROBLEMS & PESTS
Rust and slugs are possible problems.

T. 'Maple Leaf'

The starry flowers cluster along the long stems, looking like festive sparklers.

T. cordifolia

Foxglove

Digitalis

Height: 60–150 cm (24–60") **Spread:** 60 cm (24")
Flower colour: pink, purple, yellow, maroon, red, white
Blooms: summer **Hardiness:** semi-hardy

Foxgloves have a translucent beauty. Pause to look up inside the tubular flowers and discover the freckles and spots that decorate the inside. These plants self-seed happily in the garden and often pop up in new combinations with other perennials. I enjoyed pink foxgloves blooming next to a catmint plant in my garden, an attractive pairing that happened purely by accident.

The extremely poisonous nature of foxglove has been known to cause rashes, headaches and nausea simply from touching the plant.

PLANTING

Seeding: Direct sow in garden or start in cold frame in early spring. Flowers are unlikely the first year.
Planting out: Spring.
Spacing: 45–60 cm (18–24") apart.

GROWING

Foxgloves grow well in **partial or light shade**. Soil should be **fertile, humus rich, moist** and **acidic**. These plants adapt to most soils that are neither too wet nor too dry. You may wish to deadhead foxgloves once they have finished flowering, but it is a good idea to leave some of the spikes in place to spread seeds to allow for new plants. Division is unnecessary because these plants will not live long enough to be divided. They continue to occupy your garden by virtue of their ability to self-seed.

TIPS

Foxgloves are another must-have for the cottage garden or for those people interested in heritage plants. They make an excellent vertical accent along the back of a border. They are also an interesting addition to a woodland garden. Some staking may be required if the plants are in a windy location. Remove the tallest spike and the side shoots will bloom on shorter stalks that may not need staking.

Foxgloves can be grown as an annual from purchased plants if they are not winter hardy in your garden.

If too many foxgloves are growing, then you may wish to thin them out or transplant some to another location—perhaps into a friend's garden.

RECOMMENDED
D. purpurea forms a basal rosette of foliage from which tall flowering spikes emerge, growing 60–150 cm (24–60") tall and spreading 60 cm (24"). Flowers come in a wide range of colours. The insides of the flowers are often spotted with contrasting colours. **'Alba'** bears white flowers. **'Apricot'** bears apricot pink flowers. **Excelsior Hybrids,** available in many colours, bear dense spikes of flowers. **Foxy Hybrids,** which come in a range of colours, are considered dwarf by foxglove standards but easily reach 90 cm (36") in height.

ALTERNATE SPECIES
D. x mertonensis (Strawberry Foxglove) is a true perennial, unlike most foxglove cultivars, which are generally biennials. It bears rose-pink flowers and grows 90–120 cm (36–48") tall.

The hybrid varieties become less vigorous with time and self-sown seedlings may not come true to type. Sprinkle new seed in your foxglove bed each spring to ensure a steady show from the lovely flowers.

PROBLEMS & PESTS
Anthracnose, fungal leaf spot, powdery mildew, root rot, stem rot, aphids, Japanese beetles and mealybugs are possible problems for foxgloves.

The heart medication digitalis is made from extracts of foxglove. For over 200 years foxglove has been used for treating heart failure.

Geum
Geum

Height: 30–60 cm (12–24") **Spread:** 30–60 cm (12–24")
Flower colour: orange, red, yellow **Blooms:** summer
Hardiness: semi-hardy

*T*hese attractive, mounding plants bear cheerful, bright flowers for most of the summer. The plants may flag a bit during the heat of summer but are quick to revive and pick up the blooming pace as cooler weather heralds the end of summer. These plants will find a place in more gardens as their easy ways and plentiful flowers earn them the popularity they deserve.

PLANTING
Seeding: Direct sow freshly ripened seeds in fall or mid-spring.
Planting out: Spring or fall.
Spacing: 30–60 cm (12–24") apart.

GROWING

Geums prefer **full sun** but don't like excessive heat. Soil should be **fertile, evenly moist** and **well drained**. Geums do not like water-logged soil. Place gravel in the bottom of the planting hole to improve drainage. Divide geums every year or two in spring or fall to increase longevity.

TIPS

Geums make a bright-flowered addition to the border. They look particularly attractive when combined with plants that have dark blue or purple flowers.

Cut off spent flowers to keep more coming.

RECOMMENDED

G. coccineum (*G.* x *borisii*) (Scarlet Avens) forms a mounded clump. It grows 30–60 cm (12–24") tall, with an equal spread. Scarlet-red flowers are borne from late spring to late summer. **'Prince of Orange'** bears bright orange flowers until mid-summer.

G. quellyon (*G. chiloense*) (Chilean Avens) forms a clump 40–60 cm (16–24") tall, with an equal spread. It bears bright scarlet flowers all summer. **'Lady Stratheden'** has bright yellow flowers. **'Mrs. Bradshaw'** bears dark orange semi-double flowers.

PROBLEMS & PESTS

Possible problems can be caused by downy mildew, powdery mildew, fungal leaf spot, leaf smut and caterpillars.

G. coccineum

There are species of geum found in mountainous regions all over the world.

G. quellyon

Goat's Beard

Aruncus

Height: 15–180 cm (6–72") **Spread:** 30–180 cm (12–72")
Flower colour: cream, white **Blooms:** early to mid-summer
Hardiness: hardy

*A*round a pond, next to a stream or waterfall, or in a bog garden, Goat's Beard will soften any bare edges. Despite its imposing size, it has a soft and delicate appearance with its divided foliage and large, plumy, cream flowers. The Dwarf Korean Goat's Beard forms a delicate mound of shapely green leaves and loosely clustered flowers on long spikes and is only a fraction of the size of its larger cousin.

PLANTING

Seeding: Use fresh seed. Keep soil moist and conditions humid. Soil temperature should be 21–24° C (70–75° F).
Planting out: Spring or fall.
Spacing: 45–180 cm (18–72") apart.

GROWING

Goat's Beard prefers to grow in **partial to full shade**. If planted in a deep shade location, the plant will have fewer blooms. It will also tolerate full sun as long as the soil is kept evenly moist. Soil should be **rich** and **moist**, with **plenty of humus** mixed in. Goat's Beard tends to self-seed, but it is recommended to remove the spent flowers to maintain the attractive appearance of the plant and encourage a longer blooming period. Division should be done in spring or fall. Goat's Beard may be quite difficult to divide because it develops a thick root mass. Use a sharp knife to cut the root mass into pieces.

Goat's Beard looks a bit like Astilbe and is often grouped with this smaller plant to create an interesting contrast in size.

TIPS

This plant looks very natural growing along the edge of a woodland or in an open forest. It may be used at the back of a border or alongside a stream or pond.

Goat's Beard has both female and male plants, both bearing flowers. The male flowers are full and fuzzy while the female flowers are pendulous.

If you want to start some new plants from seed, then allow the seedheads to ripen before removing them. Keep in mind that you will need to have both male and female plants in order to produce seeds that will sprout.

Don't save male flowerheads—they will not produce seeds.

RECOMMENDED

A. aethusifolius (Dwarf Korean Goat's Beard) forms a low-growing, compact mound. It grows 15–40 cm (6–16") tall and spreads up to 30 cm (12"). Branched spikes of loosely held cream flowers are produced in early summer. This plant looks similar to astilbe and is sometimes sold by that name.

A. dioicus forms a large, bushy, shrub-like perennial. It grows 90–180 cm (36–72") tall, with an equal spread. Large plumes of cream white

flowers are borne from early to mid-summer. There are several cultivars, though they can be hard to find. **'Kneiffii'** is a dainty cultivar with finely divided leaves and arching stems with nodding plumes. It grows about 90 cm (36") tall and spreads 45 cm (18"). **'Zweiweltkind'** ('Child of Two Worlds') is a compact plant with drooping, white flowers. **Var. *astilbioides*** is a dwarf variety that grows only 60 cm (24") tall.

PROBLEMS & PESTS
Occasional problems with fly larvae and tarnished plant bugs are possible.

Goutweed
Bishop's Goutweed
Aegopodium

Height: 20–60 cm (8–24") **Spread:** indefinite
Flower colour: white, but inconspicuous; grown for foliage
Blooms: summer **Hardiness:** hardy

*I*n the warmer south of Ontario many gardeners shudder at the thought of this invasive groundcover taking over the garden, but in colder areas and spots where nothing else will grow, this plant can be a real blessing. From deep, dry shade to hot, exposed banks, this plant will thrive. It can be used successfully between the driveway and the house, along a street median or in the colder north where many other groundcovers can't grow.

PLANTING
Seeding: Not recommended.
Planting out: Spring, summer, fall.
Spacing: 30–60 cm (12–24").

GROWING
Goutweed grows well in any light conditions from **full sun** to **full shade**. Soil of **poor fertility** is recommended to curb invasiveness, but any **well-drained** soil is fine. This plant is drought tolerant. Division is rarely required, but you will have to dig up any parts of the plant that are venturing into undesired areas.

TIPS
Though this groundcover plant can be used almost anywhere, it is best to plant it either where it has lots of room to spread or is restricted from spreading. Good places include steep banks that are difficult to mow, in the dry shade under a tree where nothing else will grow, in planters or where a natural barrier is created such as the area between a house, walkway and driveway.

If the foliage starts to look bedraggled during summer, you can cut the plants back completely—even mow them down—and they will sprout fresh new growth.

This invasive plant thrives on neglect. This makes it an excellent choice for growing at a cottage or other infrequently used property, where there isn't much time to maintain a lawn. Avoid planting this perennial near a lawn as it will quickly creep in. It is an attractive alternative to a lawn under large shade trees where the lack of light and water will be a benefit rather than a detriment to this plant.

RECOMMENDED
A. podagraria is rarely grown because it is unstoppably invasive. The cultivar **'Variegatum'** has attractive, white-margined foliage. It is reputed to be less invasive than the species, but it is still very prone to spreading if left unchecked.

PROBLEMS & PESTS
May be afflicted by leaf blight. If this occurs, cut back the damaged foliage to renew the plants.

Hardy Geranium
Cranesbill Geranium
Geranium

Height: 10–90 cm (4–36") **Spread:** 30–90 cm (12–36")
Flower colour: white, red, pink, purple or blue
Blooms: summer **Hardiness:** hardy

The beauty and diversity found among the hardy geraniums means there is one for every garden. From low and creeping to upright and bushy, the range is almost limitless. Bigroot Geranium will quickly cover territory, even in mean, lean soil. Renard's Geranium is a small, clump-forming perennial that should be planted where you can best appreciate the beautiful, velvety leaves. Many geraniums, including 'Johnson's Blue,' are excellent petticoat plants, forming neat spreading mounds of foliage and flowers at the bases of larger shrubs and perennials, hiding potentially unsightly ankles and legs. Many geraniums develop vibrant fall colour.

PLANTING

Seeding: Species are easy to start from seed in early fall or spring. Cultivars and hybrids may not come true to type.
Planting out: Spring or fall.
Spacing: 30–60 cm (12–24") apart.

GROWING

Hardy geraniums prefer to grow in **partial or light shade** but will tolerate full sun. Soil of **average fertility** and with **good drainage** is preferred, but most conditions are tolerated except waterlogged soil. These plants dislike hot weather. Shear back spent blooms for a second set of flowers. Prune back foliage in late summer, if it is looking ratty, to rejuvenate. Divisions should be done in spring.

G. s. var. striatum

TIPS

These long-flowering plants are great in the border, filling in the spaces between shrubs and other larger plants and keeping the weeds down. They can be included in rock gardens and woodland gardens and mass planted as groundcovers.

RECOMMENDED

G. cinereum (Greyleaf Geranium) forms a basal rosette of grey-green foliage. It grows 10–15 cm (4–6") tall and spreads about 30 cm (12"). It produces small clusters of white or pink-veined flowers in early summer. It is often grown in rock gardens and other well-drained spots. **'Ballerina'** has silvery foliage and flowers darkly veined in purple.

G. s. var. striatum

G. sanguineum

G. 'Johnson's Blue' forms a spreading mat of foliage. It grows 30–45 cm (12–18") tall and spreads about 75 cm (30"). Bright blue flowers are borne over a long period in summer.

G. macrorrhizum (Bigroot Geranium, Scented Cranesbill) forms a spreading mound. It grows 30–50 cm (12–20") tall and spreads 40–60 cm (16–24"). Flowers in variable shades of pink are borne in spring and early summer. **'Album'** bears white flowers in summer on compact plants. **'Bevan's Variety'** bears magenta flowers.

G. x oxonianum is a vigorous, mound-forming plant with attractive evergreen foliage; it bears pink flowers from spring to fall. It grows up to 75 cm (30") tall and spreads about 60 cm (24"). **'A. T. Johnson'** bears many silvery-pink flowers. **'Wargrave Pink'** is a very vigorous cultivar. It grows 60 cm (24") tall, spreads about 90 cm (36"), and bears salmon pink flowers.

G. pratense (Meadow Cranesbill) forms an upright clump, growing 60–90 cm (24–36") tall and spreading about 60 cm (24"). Many white, blue or light purple flowers are borne for a short period in early summer. It self-seeds freely. **'Mrs. Kendall Clarke'** bears rose pink flowers with blue-grey veining. **'Plenum Violaceum'** bears purple double flowers for a longer period than the species because it sets no seed.

G. renardii (Renard's Geranium) forms a clump of velvety, deeply veined, crinkled foliage. A few purple-veined white flowers are borne over summer, but the foliage is the main attraction. It grows about 30 cm (12") tall, with an equal spread.

G. sanguineum (Bloody Cranesbill, Bloodred Cranesbill) forms a dense, mounding clump. It grows 15–30 cm (6–12") tall and spreads 30–60 cm (12–24"). Bright magenta flowers are borne mostly in early summer and sporadically until fall. **'Album'** has white flowers and a more open habit than other cultivars. **'Alpenglow'** has bright rosy-red flowers and dense foliage. **'Elsbeth'** has light pink flowers with dark pink veins. The foliage turns bright red in fall. **'Shepherd's Warning'** is a dwarf plant growing to 15 cm (6") tall with rosy pink flowers. **Var. *striatum*** is heat and drought tolerant. It has pale pink blooms with blood red veins.

PROBLEMS & PESTS
Rare problems with leaf spot and rust can occur.

G. pratense

G. x oxonianum

Hens and Chicks
Roof Houseleek
Sempervivum

Height: 8–15 cm (3–6") **Spread:** 30 cm (12") to indefinite
Flower colour: red, yellow, white, purple
Blooms: summer **Hardiness:** hardy to semi-hardy

*I*confess I was once an uninformed snob when it came to Hens and Chicks. I found the sight of those little green plants, plastered like Brussels sprouts in rock gardens, very glum. Then I stumbled upon a smorgasbord of hybrid Hens and Chicks cultivated by a hobby hybridizer. The colours and choices were astonishing, with leaves of red, maroon, steel grey and blue. They were crammed together on tables, and the overall effect reminded me of the muted colours of a faded tapestry.

PLANTING
Seeding: Not recommended. Remove and replant young rosettes to propagate.
Planting out: Spring.
Spacing: 25–30 cm (10–12") apart.

GROWING

Grow these plants in **full sun** or **partial shade**. Soil should be **poor to average** and **very well drained**. Add fine gravel or grit to the soil to provide adequate drainage. Once a plant blooms, it dies. When you deadhead the faded flower, pull up the soft parent plant as well. The whole plant may be left in place and the old rosettes removed periodically to provide space for the new daughter rosettes that sprout up, seemingly by magic. Divide by removing new rosettes and rooting them.

TIPS

These plants make excellent additions to rock gardens and rock walls, where they will even grow right on the rocks. Hens and Chicks can grow on almost any surface—in the past they were grown on tile roofs, and it was believed they would protect the house from lightning.

RECOMMENDED

S. tectorum forms a low-growing mat of fleshy-leaved rosettes. Each rosette is about 15–25 cm (6–10") across, but they quickly produce small rosettes that grow and multiply to fill almost any space. Flowers may be produced in summer but are not as common in colder climates. **'Atropurpureum'** has dark reddish-purple leaves. **'Limelight'** has yellow-green, pink-tipped foliage. **'Pacific Hawk'** has dark red leaves that are edged with silvery hairs.

ALTERNATE SPECIES

S. arachnoideum (Cobweb Houseleek) is identical to *S. tectorum* except that the tips of the leaves are entwined with hairy fibres, giving the appearance of cobwebs. This plant is semi-hardy in Ontario and may need protection during wet weather.

PROBLEMS & PESTS

Hens and Chicks are generally pest free, although some problems with rust and root rot can occur.

Hollyhock

Alcea

Height: 60–270 cm (24–108") **Spread:** 30–60 cm (12–24")
Flower colour: yellow, white, apricot, pink, red, purple, reddish black
Blooms: summer, sometimes into early fall **Hardiness:** hardy

*E*ngraved in my memory is the sight of a velvety, nearly black Hollyhock flower, blooming against an abandoned factory in Cleveland. Hollyhocks add a touch of romance wherever they grow. These old-fashioned plants continue to persist around old country homes and deserted city lots where they may have been planted generations ago. Their self-seeding ways earn them the title of perennial though officially they are referred to as biennials.

The powdered roots of plants in the mallow family, to which Hollyhock belongs, were once used to make a soft lozenge for sore throats. Though popular around the campfire, marshmallows no longer contain the throat-soothing properties they originally did.

PLANTING

Seeding: Direct sow in fall or start indoors in mid-winter. Either way, flowers should be produced the first summer. Plants started in spring or summer should flower the following summer.
Planting out: Spring or fall.
Spacing: 60–90 cm (24–36").

GROWING

Hollyhocks prefer **full sun** and tolerate partial shade. Soil should be of **average to high fertility**. Collect seeds or remove basal plantlets and move them to new locations each year to have a healthy display of Hollyhocks every year.

To propagate cultivars that don't come true to type from self-sown seed, carefully detach the small daughter plants that develop around the base of the plant and replant them. Division is unnecessary for these short-lived perennials.

TIPS

Choose a sheltered location that is protected from strong winds. Use Hollyhocks as background plants or in the centre of an island bed. Against a fence or wall they will be sheltered and supported. Stake the plants in a windy location.

Hollyhocks will be shorter and bushier if the main stem is pinched out early in the season. The flowers will be smaller, but the plant will have more numerous, shorter flower stems and will be less likely to be broken by the wind and can therefore be left unstaked.

Old-fashioned Hollyhocks commonly have single flowers and grow very tall. The main advantage with older varieties is the high resistance to disease. Rotate the planting site of your Hollyhocks each year or two to keep rust problems at bay.

RECOMMENDED

A. rosea is a short-lived perennial that bears flowers on tall spikes. It reappears in the garden by virtue of being a prolific self-seeder. It grows 90–270 cm (36–108") tall and about 30 cm (12") wide. From mid- or late summer to fall, it bears flowers in shades of yellow, white, pink or

purple. **'Chater's Double'** bears ruffled double flowers in many bright and pastel shades. This cultivar grows 180–240 cm (72–96") tall and is more consistently perennial than the species. **'Majorette'** is a popular dwarf cultivar. It grows 60–90 cm (24–36") tall. The semi-double flowers are in shades of yellow, white, red and apricot pink. **'Nigra'** bears single flowers in a unique shade of dark reddish black, with yellow throats. **'Summer Carnival'** is an early blooming, double-flowered cultivar with flowers in a wide range of colours.

'Chater's Double'

'Nigra'

PROBLEMS & PESTS

Hollyhock rust is the worst problem, but these plants can also have trouble with leaf spot, mallow flea beetles, aphids, slugs, Japanese beetles and cutworms when the plants are young.

Hollyhock was originally grown as a food plant. The leaves were added to salads.

Hosta
Plantain Lily
Hosta

Height: 10–90 cm (4–36") **Spread:** 30–120 cm (12–48")
Flower colour: white or purple **Blooms:** summer and fall
Hardiness: hardy

With so many gardeners facing the challenges of gardening in the shade, it's no wonder the beautiful hostas have become the best-selling perennials in North America. Breeders are always looking for new variations in the foliage. Swirls, stripes, puckers and ribs enhance the various sizes, shapes and colours of leaves. The range of hostas that are tolerant of sun and resistant to slugs increases each year. As specimen plants or in harmonious unions with other plants, hostas have a place in every garden.

PLANTING
Seeding: Direct sow or start in cold frame in spring. Young plants can take three or more years to reach flowering size.
Planting out: Spring.
Spacing: 30–90 cm (12–36") apart.

GROWING

Hostas prefer **light shade** or **partial shade** but tolerate full shade. Some will even tolerate full sun. Morning sun is preferable to afternoon sun. Soil should be **fertile, moist** and **well drained**, but most soils are tolerated. Hostas are fairly drought tolerant, especially if given a mulch to help retain moisture. Division is not required but can be done every few years in spring or summer to propagate any attractive cultivars you want more of.

TIPS

Hostas make wonderful woodland plants, looking very attractive when combined with ferns and other fine-textured plants. Hostas are also good to use in a mixed border, particularly when used to hide the ugly, leggy lower stems and branches of some shrubs. Hostas' dense growth and thick shade-providing leaves make them excellent for suppressing weeds.

Hosta flowers are attractive and often fragrant. However, the flower colour often clashes with the leaves, which are the main decorative feature of the plant. If you don't like the look of the flowers, feel free to remove them before they open—this will not harm the plant.

RECOMMENDED

Hostas have been subjected to a great deal of cross breeding and hybridizing, resulting in hundreds of cultivars, many whose exact parentage is uncertain. The cultivars below have been grouped with the most generally accepted parent species.

H. fortunei (Fortune's Hosta) is the parent of many hybrids and cultivars. It has broad dark green foliage and bears lavender-purple flowers in midsummer. It quickly forms a dense clump of foliage, growing 30–60 cm (12–24") tall and spreading 60–90 cm (24–36"). **'Albomarginata'** has variable cream or white margins on the leaves. **'Aureomarginata'** has yellow-margined leaves and is more tolerant of sun than many cultivars. **'Francee'** is often

listed without a species. It has puckered, dark green leaves with a narrow white margin.

H. plantaginea (Fragrant Hosta) has glossy bright green leaves with distinctive veins; it grows 45–75 cm (18–30") tall, spreads to about 90 cm (36") and bears large, white, fragrant flowers in late summer. **'Aphrodite'** has white double flowers. **'Honeybells'** has sweetly fragrant, light purple flowers. **'Royal Standard'** is durable and low-growing. It grows 10–20 cm (4–8") tall and spreads up to 90 cm (36"). The dark green leaves are deeply veined, and the flowers are light purple.

H. sieboldiana (Siebold's Hosta) forms a large, impressive clump of blue-green foliage. It grows about 90 cm (36") tall and spreads up to 120 cm (48"). Early-summer flowers are a light greyish purple that fade to white. **'Blue Angel'** has wavy blue-green foliage and white flowers. **'Elegans'** (var. *elegans*) has deeply puckered, blue-grey foliage and

light purple flowers. It was first introduced to gardens in 1905 and is still popular today. **'Frances Williams'** ('Yellow Edge') has puckered blue-green leaves with yellow-green margins. **'Great Expectations'** has pale yellow or cream leaves with wide, irregular, blue-green margins.

H. sieboldii (Seersucker Hosta) has undulating, narrow, green leaves with white margins. In late summer and early fall it bears light purple flowers with darker purple veins inside. It grows 30–75 cm (12–30") tall and spreads about 50–60 cm (20–24"). **'Alba'** has light green leaves with undulating margins and white flowers. **'Kabitan'** has narrow, bright yellow foliage with undulating green margins. This compact cultivar grows about 20 cm (8") tall and spreads 30 cm (12").

PROBLEMS & PESTS
Slugs, snails, leaf spot, crown rot and chewing insects such as black vine weevils are all possible problems for hostas.

Hostas are considered by some gardeners to be the ultimate in shade plants. They are available in a wide variety of leaf shapes, colours and textures.

great choice!

Iris

Iris

Height: 10–120 cm (4–48") **Spread:** 15–120 cm (6–48")
Flower colour: many shades of pink, red, purple, blue, white, brown or yellow
Blooms: spring, summer **Hardiness:** hardy to semi-hardy

P art of the magnetic charm of irises is their fleeting beauty in the garden. They force us to interrupt our daily routine and set aside our obligations to enjoy the gorgeous blooms before they fade. In a friend's garden I saw a wonderful combination of Japanese Iris, poppies and Annual Painted Sage, all blending like the colours in a Monet painting.

PLANTING

Seeding: Not recommended. Germination is erratic and hybrids and cultivars may not come true to type.
Planting out: Late summer or early fall.
Spacing: 5–120 cm (2–48") apart.

GROWING

Irises prefer to grow in **full sun** but will tolerate very light or dappled shade. Soil should be **average** or **fertile** and **well drained**. Japanese Iris and Siberian Iris prefer a moist, well-drained soil. Divide in late summer or early fall.

TIPS

Irises are popular border plants, but Japanese Iris and Siberian Iris are also useful alongside a stream or pond, and dwarf cultivars make attractive additions to rock gardens.

It is a good idea to wash your hands after handling these plants because they can cause severe internal irritation if ingested. Make sure they are not planted close to places where children play.

RECOMMENDED

I. ensata (*I. kaempferi*) (Japanese Iris) is a water-loving species. It grows up to 90 cm (36") tall and spreads about 45 cm (18"). White, blue, purple or pink flowers are borne from early to mid-summer. It rarely needs dividing. This species is not susceptible to iris borers.

I. germanica (Bearded Iris) produces flowers in all colours. This iris has been used as the parent plant for many desirable cultivars. Cultivars may vary in height and width from 15 cm to 120 cm (6" to 48"). Flowering periods range from mid-spring to mid-summer and some cultivars flower again in fall.

I. reticulata (Netted Iris) forms a small clump 10–25 cm (4–10") tall. This semi-hardy iris bears flowers in various shades of blue and purple. These

I. germanica

The iris is depicted on the wall of an Egyptian temple dating from 1500 BC, making it one of the oldest cultivated flowers.

plants grow from bulbs and can be left undis-
turbed. Bulbs may divide naturally and plants may
not flower again until the bulbs get big enough.

I. sibirica (Siberian Iris) is more resistant to iris
borers than other species. It grows 60–120 cm
(24–48") tall and 90 cm (36") wide. It flowers in
early summer; cultivars are available in many
shades, mostly purple, blue and white.

PROBLEMS & PESTS

Several problems are quite common to irises. Close observation will prevent these problems from becoming severe. Iris borers are a lethal problem. They burrow their way down the leaf until they reach the root where they continue eating until there is no root left at all. The tunnels they make in the leaves are easy to spot, and if infected leaves are removed and destroyed or the borers squished within the leaf, the borers will never reach the roots.

Leaf spot is another problem that can be controlled by removing and destroying infected leaves. Be sure to give the plants the correct growing conditions. Too much moisture for some species will allow rot diseases to settle in and kill the plants. Slugs, snails and aphids may also cause some trouble.

Powdered iris root, called orris, smells like violets when crushed and was added to perfumes and potpourris as a fixative.

I. sibirica

NO! horrible self seeds!

Jacob's Ladder
Polemonium

Height: 20–90 cm (8–36") **Spread:** 20–40 cm (8–16")
Flower colour: purple, white or blue
Blooms: late spring and summer **Hardiness:** hardy

Jacob's Ladder has long been admired for its blue-purple flowers and orderly foliage. With the introduction of 'Brise d'Anjou' it has attained a new exalted status. 'Brise d'Anjou' has ferny leaves that are brightly edged in cream. This cultivar is a standout plant for shady sections of the garden; avoid areas where hot afternoon sun can burn the foliage.

PLANTING
Seeding: Start seed in spring or fall. Keep soil temperature at about 21° C (70°-F). Seed can take up to a month to germinate.
Planting out: Spring.
Spacing: About 30 cm (12") apart.

GROWING

Jacob's Ladder species grow equally well in **full sun** or **partial shade**. Soil should be **fertile, humus rich, moist** and **well drained**. Deadhead regularly to prolong blooming. These plants self-seed readily. Division is rarely required but should be done in late summer if desired.

TIPS

Include Jacob's Ladder plants in borders and woodland gardens. *P. reptans* can be used in rock gardens and to edge paths. *P. caeruleum* can be used as a tall focal point in planters.

'Brise d'Anjou'

P. caeruleum

RECOMMENDED

P. caeruleum (Jacob's Ladder) forms a dense clump of basal foliage. Leafy upright stems are topped with clusters of purple flowers. This plant grows 45–90 cm (18–30") tall and spreads about 30 cm (12"). The leaflets of the foliage are organized in a neat, dense, ladder-like formation, giving the plant its common name. **Var.** *album* has white flowers. '**Apricot Delight'** produces many mauve flowers with apricot-pink centres. '**Brise d'Anjou'** has cream white leaflet margins but does not bear as many flowers as the species.

P. reptans (Creeping Jacob's Ladder) is a mounding perennial, 20–40 cm (8–16") tall, with an equal spread. It bears small blue or lilac flowers in late spring and early summer.

PROBLEMS & PESTS

Powdery mildew, leaf spot and rust are occasional problems.

Lady's Mantle

Alchemilla

Height: 8–45 cm (3–18") **Spread:** 50–60 cm (20–24")
Flower colour: yellow, green **Blooms:** early summer to early fall
Hardiness: hardy, semi-hardy

L ady's Mantle falls in and out of gardening fashion; with the current interest in perennials, it has once again become a garden favourite. There is something special and mysterious about this plant with its soft, scalloped leaves that catch drops of water and turn them into sparkling crystals. The foamy clusters of yellow-green flowers outweigh the stems that hold them, causing them to bend towards the ground. These soft and soothing plants can be planted along paths, under trees, in containers and anywhere else that needs a break from riotous summer colour.

PLANTING

Seeding: Direct sow fresh seed into garden, or start in containers. Transplant into garden while seedlings are small.
Planting out: Spring.
Spacing: 60 cm (24").

GROWING

Lady's Mantle will grow best in **light shade** or **partial shade**, with protection from the afternoon sun. This plant dislikes hot locations. Soil should be **fertile, humus rich, moist**, and **well drained**. Lady's Mantle is drought resistant once it is established. Division is rarely required but can be done in spring before flowering starts or in fall once flowering is complete. If more plants are desired, move some of the self-seeded plants that are bound to show up to where you want them.

A. mollis

Poets and alchemists were inspired by the crystal-like dew that collects on the leaves, which was reputed to have magical and medicinal qualities.

A. mollis

A. mollis

A. alpina

TIPS

Lady's Mantle is ideal for grouping under trees in woodland gardens and along border edges where it softens the bright colours of other plants. A wonderful location is alongside a pathway that winds through a lightly wooded area.

If your Lady's Mantle begins to look tired and heat-stressed during summer, rejuvenate it by trimming it back so new foliage can fill in.

RECOMMENDED

A. alpina (Alpine Lady's Mantle) is a diminutive, low-growing plant that has soft white hairs on the backs of the leaves, giving the appearance of a silvery margin to each leaf. Clusters of tiny yellow flowers are borne in summer. It grows 8–13 cm (3–5") tall and spreads up to 50 cm (20").

A. mollis (Common Lady's Mantle) is the most frequently grown species. It forms a mound of soft, rounded foliage. Sprays of yellowish-green flowers held above the foliage may be borne from early summer to early fall. It grows 20–45 cm (8–18") tall and spreads up to about 60 cm (24").

PROBLEMS & PESTS

Lady's Mantle plants rarely suffer from any problems, though fungus may be a problem during warm, wet summers.

The flowers can be enjoyed in fresh or dried arrangements and the leaves can be boiled to make a green dye for wool.

A. alpina

A. mollis

Lamb's Ears
Woolly Betony
Stachys

Height: 15–45 cm (6–18") **Spread:** 45–60 cm (18–24")
Flower colour: pink, purple **Blooms:** summer
Hardiness: hardy to semi-hardy

*L*amb's Ears can be used effectively to break up monotonous carpets of green and to provide a silvery background for brightly coloured flowers. The newer variety 'Big Ears' is a very useful, attractive addition to the garden with larger leaves and a clump-forming habit. It does not have the silvery sheen of the species but still produces good texture for the garden.

PLANTING
Seeding: Direct sow or start in containers in cold frame in spring.
Planting out: Spring.
Spacing: 45–60 cm (18–24").

GROWING

Lamb's ears grows best in **full sun**. Soil should be of **poor or average fertility** and **well drained**. Leaves can rot in humid weather if the soil is poorly drained. Remove spent flower spikes to keep plants looking neat. Select a flowerless cultivar if you don't want to deadhead. Divide in spring.

TIPS

Lamb's Ears makes a great ground-cover in a new garden where the soil has not yet been amended. As long as good drainage is provided, Lamb's Ears will do well. It can be used to edge borders and pathways, providing a soft, silvery backdrop for more vibrant colours in the border.

Lamb's Ears is a low-maintenance plant.

RECOMMENDED

S. byzantina (*S. lanata*) forms a mat of thick, woolly rosettes of leaves. It grows 15–45 cm (6–18") tall, with a spread of 45–60 cm (18–24"). Pinkish-purple flowers are borne all summer. **'Big Ears'** has purple leaves that are twice as big as those of the species. **'Silver Carpet'** has silvery white fuzzy foliage; it rarely, if ever, produces flowers.

PROBLEMS & PESTS

Fungal leaf problems including rot, powdery mildew, rust and leaf spot are rare but can occur in hot, humid weather. Diseased or damaged foliage can be cut back. New foliage will sprout when the weather cools down.

seedling

Ligularia
Ligularia

Height: 90–180 cm (36–72") **Spread:** 60–150 cm (24–60")
Flower colour: yellow or orange; has ornamental foliage
Blooms: summer, sometimes early fall **Hardiness:** semi-hardy

L igularias are stunning plants, but only in areas where they get adequate moisture and protection from afternoon sun. The best planting I've seen was at the edge of a cool woodland near a stream. They were unforgettable with tall spikes of yellow flowers like candelabras.

PLANTING

Seeding: Species can be started outdoors in spring in containers. Cultivars rarely come true to type.
Planting out: Spring.
Spacing: 60–150 cm (24–60").

GROWING

Ligularias should be grown in **light shade** or **partial shade** with protection from the afternoon sun. Full sun is actually preferred but only in consistently moist soil. Soil should be of **average fertility, humus rich** and **moist**. Division is rarely, if ever, required but can be done in spring or fall to propagate a desirable cultivar.

'Desdemona'

L. dentata

'The Rocket'

TIPS

Use ligularias alongside a pond or stream. They can also be used in a well-watered border or naturalized in a moist meadow or woodland garden. The foliage can wilt in hot sun, even in moist soil. The leaves will revive at night, but this won't help how horrible they look during the day. In this situation it is best to move the plant to a cooler, more shaded position in the garden.

RECOMMENDED

L. dentata (Bigleaf Ligularia, Golden Groundsel) forms a clump of rounded, heart-shaped leaves. It grows 90–150 cm (36–60") tall and spreads 90–120 cm (36–48"). In summer and early fall it bears clusters of orange-yellow flowers, held above the foliage. **'Desdemona'** and **'Othello'** are two similar cultivars. They have orange flowers and purple-green foliage. They come fairly true to type when grown from seed.

'The Rocket'

L. przewalskii (Shevalski's Ligularia) also forms a clump but has deeply incised leaves. It grows 120–180 cm (48–72") tall and spreads 60–120 cm (24–48"). In mid- and late summer it produces yellow flowers on long purple spikes.

L. stenocephala (Narrow-spiked Ligularia) has toothed rather than incised foliage and bears bright yellow flowers on dark purple-green spikes. It grows 90–150 cm (36–60") in height and width. This species is closely related to the previous one, and **'The Rocket'** may be a hybrid of the two. This cultivar has heart-shaped leaves with ragged-toothed margins. The leaf veins are dark, becoming purple at the leaf base.

PROBLEMS & PESTS
Ligularias have no serious problems, though slugs can cause damage to young foliage.

L. dentata

L. dentata

Lily-of-the-Valley
Convallaria

Height: 15–30 cm (6–12") **Spread:** indefinite
Flower colour: white, pink **Blooms:** spring
Hardiness: hardy

For such a sweet and delicate looking plant, Lily-of-the-valley can be an invasive bully, pushing its way in everywhere and overwhelming less vigorous plants. Gardeners are very forgiving of this habit in spring, when Lily-of-the-valley blooms. Perfectly bell-shaped, richly perfumed flowers remind us of why we planted Lily-of-the-valley in the first place. I was fortunate to purchase a clump with unusual striped foliage at the Royal Botanical Gardens annual plant sale. Now I enjoy my Lily-of-the-valley all summer and not just while it is in flower.

PLANTING

Seeding: Not recommended. Very easy to propagate by division.
Planting out: Spring or fall.
Spacing: About 30 cm (12"). They will quickly spread and fill an area.

GROWING

Lily-of-the-valley will grow well in any light from **full sun** to **full shade**. Soil should be of **average fertility, humus rich,** and **moist**, but almost any soil conditions are tolerated. This plant is drought resistant. Division is rarely required but can be done whenever you need more plants for another area or to donate to someone else's garden. The pairs of leaves grow from small pips, or eyes, that form along the root. Divide a length of root into pieces, leaving at least one pip on each piece.

TIPS

This versatile groundcover can be grown in a variety of locations. It is a beautiful plant to naturalize in woodland gardens, perhaps bordering a pathway or beneath shade trees where little else will grow. It also makes a good groundcover in a shrub border where the dense growth and fairly shallow roots will keep the weeds down but won't interfere with the shrubs.

Lily-of-the-valley can be quite invasive. It is a good idea not to grow it with plants that are less vigorous and likely to be overwhelmed, such as alpine plants in a rock garden. Give Lily-of-the-valley plants plenty of space to grow and leave them to it. Avoid planting them where you may later spend all your time trying to get rid of them.

Lily-of-the-valley is well known for the delightful scent of its flowers. In fall, dig up a few roots and plant them into pots. Keep the pots in a sheltered section of the garden, such a window well, cold frame or unheated porch, for the winter. In early spring you can bring the pots indoors and enjoy the flowers and their scent.

RECOMMENDED

C. majalis forms a mat of foliage. It grows 15–25 cm (6–10") tall and spreads indefinitely. Small arching stems lined with fragrant, white,

European legend claims the origin of Lily-of-the-valley to be either the tears of the Virgin Mary shed at the cross or the tears of Mary Magdalen shed at Christ's tomb.

bell-shaped flowers are produced in spring. **'Albostriata'** and **'Aureovariegata'** have white- or yellow-striped leaves, respectively. **'Flore Pleno'** has white double flowers and tends not to be quite as invasive as the species. **'Fortin's Giant'** has larger leaves and flowers than the species and can grow up to 30 cm (12") tall. **'Rosea'** (var. *rosea*) has light pink or pink-veined flowers.

PROBLEMS & PESTS
Occasional problems with moulds and stem rot can occur.

Lily-of-the-valley is currently being researched for its potential medicinal qualities.

Lungwort
Pulmonaria

Height: 20–60 cm (8–24") **Spread:** 20–90 cm (8–36")
Flower colour: blue, red, pink, white **Blooms:** spring
Hardiness: hardy to semi-hardy

There is a wide array of lungworts to be experienced by gardeners. Their highly attractive foliage ranges from apple green to silver spotted, olive to dark emerald. The flowers turn different colours as they age, from pink to wine to sky blue. These plants easily share space in the garden with hostas, but are slug and pest resistant. Lungworts offer countless ways to layer the ground with texture and pattern.

There are over 20 common names for this plant. Many are after biblical characters such as Abraham, Isaac and Jacob, Adam and Eve, Children of Israel, and Virgin Mary.

PLANTING

Seeding: Don't come consistently true to type from seed. Start seed in containers outdoors in spring.
Planting out: Spring or fall.
Spacing: About 30–45 cm (12–18") apart.

GROWING

Lungworts prefer **partial shade** to **full shade**. Soil should be **fertile, humus rich, moist** and **well drained**. Rot can occur in very wet soil. Shear plants back lightly after flowering to deadhead and keep plants tidy. Divide in early summer after flowering or in fall. Provide the newly planted divisions with lots of water to help them become re-established.

TIPS

Lungworts are useful and attractive groundcover plants for shady borders, woodland gardens and edges of ponds and streams.

RECOMMENDED

P. angustifolia (Blue Lungwort) forms a mounded clump of foliage. The leaves have no spots. This plant grows 20–30 cm (8–12") tall and spreads 45–60 cm (18–24"). Clusters of bright blue flowers, held above the foliage, are borne from early to late spring.

P. longifolia (Long-leaved Lungwort) forms a dense clump of long, narrow, white-spotted, green leaves. It grows 20–24 cm (8–12") tall and spreads 20–60 cm (8–24"). It bears clusters of blue flowers in spring, often before or as the foliage emerges.

P. officinalis (Common Lungwort, Spotted Dog) forms a loose clump of evergreen foliage, spotted with white. It grows 25–30 cm (10–12") tall and spreads about 45 cm (18"). Spring flowers open pink and mature to blue. This was the species grown for its reputed medicinal properties, but it is now valued for its ornamental qualities. **'Cambridge Blue'** bears many blue flowers.

P. saccharata

P. saccharata

P. longifolia

P. saccharata

'**Sissinghurst White**' has pink buds that open to white flowers. The leaves are heavily spotted with white.

P. rubra (Red Lungwort) forms a loose clump of unspotted, softly hairy leaves. It grows 30–60 cm (12–24") tall and spreads 60–90 cm (24–36"). Bright red flowers appear in early spring. '**Redstart**' has pinkish-red flowers.

P. saccharata (Bethlehem Sage) forms a compact clump of large, white-spotted evergreen leaves. It grows 30–45 cm (12–18") tall, with a spread of about 60 cm (24"). Spring flowers may be purple, red or white. This species has given rise to many cultivars and hybrids. '**Janet Fisk**' is very heavily spotted and appears almost silvery in the garden. Pink flowers mature to blue. '**Mrs. Moon**' has pink buds that open to a light purple-blue. The leaves are dappled with silvery white spots. '**Pink Dawn**' has dark pink flowers that age to purple.

PROBLEMS & PESTS

Lungwort plants may get powdery mildew if the soil dries out for extended periods. Remove and destroy damaged leaves. These plants are generally problem free.

P. saccharata

Pulmonaria is a traditional culinary and medicinal herb. The young leaves may be added to soups and stews to flavour and thicken the broth. The spotted leaves also make an attractive addition, when dried, to potpourri.

P. saccharata

Lupine
Lupinus

Height: 45–90 cm (18–36") **Spread:** 30–45 cm (12–18")
Flower colour: white, cream, yellow, pink, red, orange, purple, blue; some bicoloured **Blooms:** early to mid-summer **Hardiness:** hardy to semi-hardy

Tall spires of lupine flowers in beautiful, varied colours give your garden a fairy-tale look. Their appearance at the end of spring heralds the bright colours of summer. Pay attention to their requirements or you may be disappointed. In suitable conditions they quickly thrive, but in poor conditions they disappear faster than spilled mercury.

Lupines are in the same plant family as beans and peas. However, the pods and seeds of lupine will cause stomach upset if ingested.

PLANTING

Seeding: Soak seeds in warm water for 24 hours then plant directly outdoors in mid-fall or mid-spring. If you start seeds indoors you may need to place planted seeds in the refrigerator for four to six weeks after soaking them.

Planting out: Spring or fall.

Spacing: About 30 cm (12") apart.

GROWING

Lupines grow best in **light shade** or **partial shade**. Soil should be of **average to high fertility, sandy, well drained** and **slightly acidic**. Protect plants from drying winds. Deadheading is recommended for lupines, to encourage more flowering as the season progresses. However, lupines may self-seed if the spent spikes are left in place. One solution is to leave just a couple of spikes in place

Russell hybrids

once flowering is finished to allow some seedlings to fill in as the older plants die out.

These perennials can be a bit short-lived. Carefully removing the small offsets that develop at the base of the plant and replanting them will provide you with more plants. Division is not required. Lupines dislike having their roots disturbed.

TIPS

Lupines are wonderful when massed together in borders or in cottage and natural gardens.

RECOMMENDED

There are many species of lupines, but they are rarely grown in eastern North American gardens in favour of the many popular hybrids. Most lupines form a dense basal mound of foliage from which tall spikes emerge, bearing many colourful pea-like flowers.

Gallery Hybrids are dwarf hybrids. They grow about 45–60 cm (18–24") tall and spread about 30–45 cm (12–18"). They are available with flowers in blue, red, pink, yellow or white.

Russell Hybrids were among the first groups of hybrids developed. They grow about 60–90 cm (24–36") tall, spread 30–45 cm (12–18") and bear flowers in a wide range of solid colours and bicolours.

PROBLEMS & PESTS

Aphids are the biggest problem for lupines. Slugs, snails, leaf spot, downy mildew, powdery mildew, rust, stem rot and damping off (in seedlings) can cause occasional trouble.

Lychnis
Maltese Cross, Rose Campion
Lychnis

Height: 60–120 cm (24–48") **Spread:** 30–45 cm (12–18")
Flower colour: magenta, white, scarlet, red
Blooms: summer **Hardiness:** hardy to semi-hardy

*T*he genus name, *Lychnis*, is from Greek and means 'lamp,' a reference to the brilliant glow of the flowers. Maltese Cross bears flowers of flaming scarlet. They are long lasting when cut and are a favourite in cottage gardens. Rose Campion bears bright magenta flowers that have long been frowned upon by fashionable gardeners who claim they clash with everything. Cultivars offer less intense colours such as white, pink and red.

PLANTING

Seeding: Start seeds in late spring. Best germination will occur if you keep the soil between 20–21° C (68–70°-F).

Planting out: Spring.

Spacing: 30–45 cm (12–18").

GROWING

Lychnis will grow equally well in **full sun** or **partial shade**. Soil should be of **average fertility** and **well drained**. These plants are quite short-lived. They do tend to self-seed, though, and will re-populate the garden with new plants as old ones die out. They re-seed easily in gravel pathways, from where young plants can be easily transplanted. Basal cuttings can also be taken to propagate the plants. Division can be done in spring, though these short-lived plants may not need it.

RECOMMENDED

L. chalcedonica (Maltese Cross) is a stiff, upright plant. It grows 90–120 cm (36–48") tall and spreads 30–45 cm (12–18"). The scarlet flowers are borne in clusters in early and mid-summer. Some support may be required to keep this plant standing upright. **'Alba'** has white flowers.

L. coronaria (Rose Campion) forms an upright mass of silvery-grey leaves and branching stems. It grows 60–90 cm (24–36") tall and about 45 cm (18") wide. The plant is dotted in late summer with magenta pink flowers, which are very striking against the silvery foliage. **'Alba'** has white flowers. **'Angel's Blush'** has white flowers with reddish-pink centres. **'Atrosanguinea'** has red flowers.

L. chalcedonica

TIPS

These tall plants may need some support, particularly in a windy location. Peony supports or twiggy branches pushed into the soil before the plants get too tall are best and are less noticeable than having the plants tied to stakes.

Lychnis species make beautiful, carefree additions to a border, cottage garden or naturalized garden.

L. coronaria

Mallow

Malva

Height: 20–120 cm (8–48") **Spread:** 30–60 cm (12–24")
Flower colour: purple, pink, white, blue **Blooms:** summer, fall
Hardiness: semi-hardy

Mallows are carefree, easy-to-grow plants that add a cheerful, relaxed air to the garden. From the loosely held spikes of pink flowers on Hollyhock Mallow to the vibrant purples of the flowers of Cheeses, these perennials are a wonderful addition to any style of garden. They seem best suited to a cottage-style garden, where they are likely to thrive with minimal care.

Mallow is reputed to have a calming effect when ingested and was used in the Middle Ages as an antidote for aphrodisiacs and love potions.

PLANTING
Seeding: Direct sow in spring or early summer.
Planting out: Spring or summer.
Spacing: 30–60 cm (12–24").

GROWING
Mallows grow well in **full sun** or **partial shade.**
Soil should be of **average fertility, moist** and **well
drained.** Mallow plants are drought tolerant. In
very rich soils the plants may require staking.
Mallow plants can be propagated by basal cuttings
taken in spring.

Mallows self-seed. Cutting plants back by about
half in late May will encourage more compact,
bushy growth but will delay flowering by a couple
of weeks. Transplant or thin out seedlings if they
are too crowded. Mallows will not need dividing.

'Bibor Felho'

M. moschata

M. moschata

TIPS
Use mallows in a mixed border or in a wild or cottage garden. Deadhead the flowers to keep the plants blooming until October.

Mallows also make good cut flowers.

RECOMMENDED
M. alcea (Hollyhock Mallow) is a loose, upright branching plant. It grows 60–120 cm (24–48") tall and spreads 45–60 cm (18–24"). This plant bears pink flowers with notched petals all summer.

M. moschata (Musk Mallow) is a bushy, upright plant with musk-scented leaves. It grows about 90 cm (36") tall, spreads about 60 cm (24") and bears pale pink or white flowers all summer. **'Pirouette'** ('Alba') bears pure white flowers.

'Primley Blue'

M. sylvestris (Cheeses) may be upright or spreading in habit. It can grow from 20–120 cm (8–48") tall and spreads about 30–60 cm (12–24"). The pink flowers have darker veining and are produced all summer. There are many cultivars of this species available. **'Bibor Felho'** has rose-purple flowers with darker purple veins. This is an upright cultivar. **'Braveheart,'** also an upright cultivar, has light purple-pink flowers with dark purple veins. **'Primley Blue'** has light purple-blue flowers. This is a prostrate cultivar and grows only about 20 cm (8") tall. **'Zebrina'** has pale pink or white flowers with purple veins. This is an upright grower.

PROBLEMS & PESTS

Problems with rust, leaf spot, Japanese beetles and spider mites can occur occasionally.

'Bibor Felho'

'Primley Blue'

Marguerite Daisy
Golden Marguerite
Anthemis

Height: 60–90 cm (24–36") **Spread:** 60-90 cm (24–36")
Flower colour: yellow, cream, white
Blooms: late spring to late summer **Hardiness:** hardy

Long-blooming Marguerite Daisy puts on a sunny display all summer. This neat plant forms a tidy mound in the garden and is suitable for both formal and informal gardens. The flowers are ideal for fresh arrangements, and, happily, frequent cutting of flowers will encourage more blooms.

PLANTING
Seeding: Direct sow in spring.
Planting out: Spring.
Spacing: 45–60 cm (18–24") apart.

GROWING
Marguerite Daisy prefers **full sun**. Soil should be of **average fertility** and should be **well drained**. This plant is drought tolerant.

Flowering tends to occur in waves. Cutting off the dead flowers will encourage continual flowering all summer. If the plant begins to look thin and spread out, you may cut it back hard to promote new growth and flowers. Marguerite Daisy clumps tend to die out in the middle and should therefore be divided every two or three years in spring or fall in order to keep them looking their best.

TIPS
Marguerite Daisy forms attractive clumps that blend wonderfully into a cottage-style garden. Their drought tolerance makes them ideal for use in rock gardens and on exposed slopes.

To avoid the need for staking, group several plants together so they can support each other. If stakes are used, then small, twiggy branches, installed while the plant is small, will support the plant and be hidden once the plant gets taller.

RECOMMENDED
A. tinctoria forms a mounded clump of foliage that is completely covered in bright or cream-yellow, daisy-like flowers in summer. **'Beauty of Grallach'** has deep orange-yellow flowers. **'E. C. Buxton'** has flowers with creamy petals and yellow centres. **'Grallach Gold'** has bright yellow-gold flowers. **'Moonlight'** has large, pale yellow flowers.

PROBLEMS & PESTS
Marguerite Daisy may suffer from such fungal problems as powdery or downy mildew, but only rarely. Aphids can be an occasional nuisance.

Meadow Rue

Thalictrum

Height: 60–150 cm (24–60") **Spread:** 30–90 cm (12–36")
Flower colour: pink, purple, yellow, white
Blooms: spring or summer **Hardiness:** hardy to semi-hardy

Meadow rues have the unique ability to add height without heft to the garden. These tall, but not overbearing, plants have fine foliage and sway gracefully in the wind. The fluffy flowers are held up on wiry stems. I recently saw a planting of *Thalictrum roche-bruneanum* 'Lavender Mist' in a woodland garden, and the lavender flowers left a lasting impression.

PLANTING

Seeding: Direct sow in fall or indoors in early spring. Keep soil temperature at about 21° C (70° F).
Planting out: Spring.
Spacing: About 30–60 cm (12–24") apart.

GROWING

Meadow rues prefer **light or partial shade** but will tolerate full sun if the soil remains moist. Soil should be **humus rich, moist** and **well drained**. These plants rarely need to be divided. If necessary for propagation, divide in spring as the foliage begins to develop. They may take a while to re-establish themselves once they have been divided or have had their roots disturbed.

'Lavender Mist'

TIPS

In the middle or at the back of a border, meadow rues make a soft backdrop for bolder plants and flowers and are beautiful when naturalized in an open woodland or meadow garden.

Meadow rue flowers are generally petal-less. The unique flowers consist of showy sepals and stamens.

'Lavender Mist'

T. aquilegifolium

These plants often do not emerge until quite late in spring. Mark the location where they are planted so that you do not inadvertently disturb the roots if you are cultivating their bed before they begin to grow.

Do not plant individual plants too close together because their stems can become tangled.

RECOMMENDED

T. aquilegifolium (Columbine Meadow Rue) forms an upright mound 60–90 cm (24–36") tall, with an equal spread. Pink or white plumes of flowers are borne in early summer. The leaves are similar in appearance to those of columbines. **'Thundercloud'** ('Purple Cloud') has dark purple flowers. **'White Cloud'** has white flowers.

T. delvayi (Yunnan Meadow Rue) forms a clump of narrow stems that usually need staking. It grows 120–150 cm (48–60") tall and spreads about 60 cm (24"). It bears fluffy purple or white flowers from mid-summer to fall. **'Album'** has

white flowers. **'Hewitt's Double'** is a popular cultivar that produces numerous tiny, purple, pompom-like flowers.

***T. rochebruneanum* 'Lavender Mist'** (Lavender Mist Meadow Rue) forms a narrow, upright clump. It grows 90–150 cm (36–60") tall and spreads 30–60 cm (12–24"). The late-summer blooms are lavender purple and have numerous distinctive yellow stamens.

PROBLEMS & PESTS
Infrequent problems with powdery mildew, rust, smut and leaf spot can occur.

T. aquilegifolium

T. aquilegifolium

Meadowsweet

Filipendula

Height: 60–240 cm (24–96") **Spread:** 45–120 cm (18–48")
Flower colour: white, cream, pink **Blooms:** late spring, summer
Hardiness: hardy

*F*or an impressive, informal, vertical accent by a pond or in a bog, meadowsweet plants are second to none. The showy, fragrant flowers are borne in fluffy clusters at the ends of the stems. The flowers develop into interesting seedheads that linger into fall. Meadowsweets are statuesque plants that are at home in wet sites.

PLANTING
Seeding: Germination can be erratic. Start seed in cold frame in fall. Keep soil evenly moist.
Planting out: Spring.
Spacing: 45–90 cm (18–36").

GROWING
Meadowsweet plants prefer **partial or light shade**. Full sun is tolerated if the soil remains sufficiently moist. Soil should be **fertile, deep, humus rich** and **moist**. Meadowsweets tend to self-seed. These plants can be deadheaded if desired, but the faded seedheads are quite attractive when left in place. Divide in spring or fall. You may need a sharp knife to divide these plants as they grow thick, tough roots. If dividing these perennials seems to be too daunting a task, you may find transplanting the seedlings to be an easier way to get new plants.

TIPS
Most meadowsweets are excellent plants for bog gardens or wet sites. Grow them alongside streams or in moist meadows. Meadowsweets may also be grown in the back of a border, as long as they are kept well watered. *F. vulgaris* prefers dry soil. It is a good choice if you have a dry area of the garden.

F. rubra

F. ulmaria *was a popular flavouring for ales and meads in medieval times. It is thought that the name meadowsweet is derived from the Anglo-Saxon word* medesweete *because it was often used to flavour mead.*

F. ulmaria

F. ulmaria

F. ulmaria (Meadowsweet, Queen-of-the-Meadow) was used in past times to flavour mead and ale. Today it is gaining popularity for its use flavouring vinegars and jams. It may also be made into a pleasant wine (made in much the same way as dandelion wine).

RECOMMENDED

F. purpurea (Japanese Meadowsweet) forms a clump of stems and large, deeply lobed foliage. It grows up to 120 cm (48") tall and spreads about 60 cm (24"). It bears pinkish-red flowers that fade to pink in late summer. **'Elegans'** has fragrant white flowers. The spent flowerheads develop a red tint, so it is not essential to deadhead.

F. rubra (Queen-of-the-Prairie) forms a large spreading clump. It grows to be 180–245 cm (72–96") tall and 120 cm (48") wide. It bears clusters of fragrant, pink flowers from early to mid-summer. **'Venusta'** bears very showy pink flowers that fade to light pink in fall.

'Flore Pleno'

F. ulmaria (Meadowsweet, Queen-of-the-Meadow) bears cream white flowers in large clusters. It grows to be 60–90 cm (24–36") tall and 60 cm (24") wide. **'Aurea'** has yellow foliage that matures to light green as summer progresses. **'Flore Pleno'** has double flowers.

F. vulgaris (Dropwort, Meadowsweet) is a low-growing species. It grows up to 60 cm (24") tall and 45 cm (18") wide. **'Rosea'** has pink flowers and **'Flore Pleno'** has white, double flowers.

PROBLEMS & PESTS
Powdery mildew, rust and leaf spot can be troublesome.

In the 16th century it was customary to strew floors with rushes and herbs to warm the floor underfoot, to freshen the air and to combat infections; meadowsweet was the herb Queen Elizabeth I preferred for this purpose.

F. rubra

Monkshood

Aconitum

Height: 90–180 cm (36–72") **Spread:** 30–45 cm (12–18")
Flower colour: purple, blue or white
Blooms: late summer **Hardiness:** hardy to semi-hardy

As much as I have tried, I have not had much luck growing monkshood plants in my hot, dry garden. Their tall spikes of blue-purple flowers are very showy in the border, but they demand a cool, moist site or they languish. Monkshoods are ideal in a bog garden or pondside planting.

Aconitum may come from the Greek akoniton, *meaning 'dart.' The ancient Chinese and the Arabs used the juice of monkshood to poison arrow tips.*

PLANTING

Seeding: Germination may be irregular. Seeds planted in garden in spring may bloom the following summer; seeds planted later will not likely bloom for yet another year.

Planting out: Spring; bare-rooted tubers may be planted in fall.

Spacing: 45 cm (18") apart.

GROWING

Monkshoods prefer to grow in **slightly shaded** areas but will tolerate sun if the climate is cool. These plants will grow in any **moist soil** but prefer to be in a **rich soil** with **lots of organic matter** worked in. Monkshoods prefer conditions to be on the cool side. They will do poorly when the weather gets hot, particularly if conditions do not cool down at night. Mulch the roots to keep them cool.

A. napellus

A. napellus

'Bicolor'

These plants require a period of dormancy in winter. Monkshoods prefer not to be divided as they may be a bit slow to re-establish themselves. If division is desired to increase the number of plants, then it should be done in late fall or early spring.

TIPS

Monkshood plants are perfect for cool, boggy locations along streams or next to ponds. They make tall and elegant additions to a woodland garden in combination with lower-growing plants.

When dividing or transplanting monkshoods, the crown of the plant should never be planted at a depth lower than where it was previously growing. Burying the crown any deeper will only cause it to rot and the plant to die.

Do not plant monkshoods near tree roots because these plants cannot compete with trees.

RECOMMENDED

A. x *bicolor* (Bicolour Monkshood) is a group of hybrids that contains several of the more popular cultivars. **'Bicolor'** bears blue and white flowers. The flower spikes are often branched. **'Bressingham Spire'** bears dark purple-blue flowers on strong spikes. It grows up to 90 cm (36") tall but needs no staking.

A. *charmichaelii* (Azure Monkshood) forms a low mound of basal leaves from which the flower spikes emerge. The foliage generally grows to about 60 cm (24") in height, but the plant can grow up to 180 cm (72") tall when in flower. Purple or blue flowers are borne from mid- to late summer, a bit later than those of other species. **'Arendsii'** bears dark blue flowers on strong spikes that need no staking.

A. *napellus* (Common Monkshood) is an erect plant that forms a basal mound of finely divided foliage. It grows 90–150 cm (36–60") tall and spreads 30–45 cm (12–18"). This plant bears dark purple-blue flowers from mid- to late summer.

All parts of this pretty plant are poisonous.

A. napellus

A. x bicolor

Mullein

Verbascum

Height: 90–180 cm (36–72")
Spread: 45–60 cm (18–24")
Flower colour: yellow, white or orange
Blooms: summer
Hardiness: semi-hardy to tender

Most gardeners have a love-hate relationship with mulleins, stemming from the weedy naturalized mulleins that turn up uninvited in the garden and then proceed to self-seed ruthlessly; each plant is capable of producing almost 200,000 seeds. The more acceptable garden varieties are a real lifesaver for gardens that are too hot and dry to successfully grow other tall, back-of-the-border plants like delphinium, lupine and monkshood. Many beautiful flowers have been developed in the hybrids, though their self-seeded offspring may not come true to type.

PLANTING

Seeding: Start seeds in containers in cold frame in late spring or early summer; may not flower until third season.
Planting out: Spring.
Spacing: 45 cm (18") apart.

GROWING

Grow these plants in **full sun**. Soil should be **poor, alkaline** and **well drained**. When planted in soil that is too rich, the plants become floppy and fall over. Mulleins will rot if planted in a location with moist soil or where water from run-off or overflowing gutters hits the foliage.

The plants are short-lived, but self-seeding will keep them growing in your garden. Removing the spent flower spikes may encourage the plants to bloom again. Mulleins may be divided in spring, though this is rarely necessary.

V. olympicum

'Helen Johnson'

TIPS

Use in the middle or at the back of a sunny border. Mulleins are also good in natural gardens.

RECOMMENDED

V. chaixii (Nettle-Leaved Mullein) grows up to 90 cm (36") tall and bears yellow flowers. **'Album'** has white flowers with mauve centres.

V. x *hybridum* is a group of hybrids generally derived by crossing *V. olympicum*, *V. phoeniceum* and other species to develop a group with more colourful flowers. They generally grow about 90–120 cm (36–48") tall. **'Cotswold Queen'** has bronzy-salmon flowers with purple centres. **'Helen Johnson'** has orange flowers. **'Mont Blanc'** has white flowers.

V. olympicum (Olympic Mullein) has very woolly, silvery-grey leaves and bright yellow flowers. It grows up to 180 cm (72") tall.

PROBLEMS & PESTS

Powdery mildew, fungal leaf spot and caterpillars may cause problems.

Some species of mullein are considered weeds. Each capsule on a flower spike can produce hundreds of seeds.

find out if they self seed

Oriental Poppy

Papaver

Height: 45–120 cm (18–48") **Spread:** 45–90 cm (18–36")
Flower colour: red, orange, pink or white
Blooms: spring and early summer **Hardiness:** hardy

A vivid scene remains with me from a garden I visited one June. Groups of Red Oriental Poppy and 'Johnson's Blue' geraniums were blooming in generous drifts, and the whole intense scene was reflected in a very still pond. The owner of the garden was a painter and the landscape reflected his vision. Oriental Poppies are heavenly in the early and mid-summer garden, and then they go dormant later in summer.

PLANTING

Seeding: Direct sow in spring or fall.
Planting out: Spring.
Spacing: 60 cm (24") apart.

GROWING

Grow these plants in a location that receives **full sun**. Soil should be **average to fertile** and must be **well drained**. Plants will die back after flowering and send up fresh new growth in late summer, which should be left in place for winter insulation. Division is rarely required but may be done in fall once the new rosettes begin to form.

Use of poppy seeds in cooking and baking can be traced as far back as the ancient Egyptians.

TIPS

Small groups of Oriental Poppy look attractive in an early summer border.

Because it goes completely dormant by mid-summer, Oriental Poppy may leave a bare spot in a border. Baby's Breath and catmint plants make good companions and will fill in any blank spots left in the border later in summer.

RECOMMENDED

P. orientale forms an upright, oval clump. It grows 45–120 cm (18–48") tall and spreads 60–90 cm (24–36"). Red, scarlet, pink or white flowers with prominent black stamens are borne in late spring and early summer. **'Allegro'** has bright scarlet-red flowers. **'Black and White'** has white flowers with black markings at the bases of the

petals. **'Pizzicato'** is a dwarf cultivar, with flowers in a wide range of colours. It forms a mound 45–60 cm (18–24") tall, with an equal spread.

PROBLEMS & PESTS

Problems with powdery mildew, leaf smut, grey mould, root rot and damping off may occur.

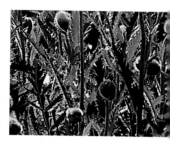

Pachysandra
Japanese Spurge
Pachysandra

Height: about 20 cm (8") **Spread:** 30–45 cm (12–18"), or more
Flower colour: white, inconspicuous; foliage plant
Blooms: early spring **Hardiness:** semi-hardy

F ans of pachysandras love the dependable way these plants blanket the ground. Combine a pachysandra with a shade-loving native plant such as Canada Wild Ginger, Meadow Anemone or some of the native violets to encourage diversity and break the monotony of a single type of ground-cover. Watch for new varieties of pachysandras to enter the market, including one with very glossy leaves.

PLANTING
Seeding: Not recommended.
Planting out: Spring or fall.
Spacing: 30–45 cm (12–18") apart.

GROWING
Pachysandras prefer **light to full shade** and tolerate partial shade. Any soil that is **moist, acidic, humus rich** and **well drained** is good. Division is not required, but can be done in spring for propagation.

TIPS
Pachysandras are durable ground-covers under trees, along north walls, in shady borders and in woodland gardens.

The foliage is considered evergreen but can look tired by spring. Remove old foliage to make way for new foliage.

RECOMMENDED
P. terminalis (Japanese Spurge) forms a low mass of foliage rosettes. It grows about 20 cm (8") tall and can spread almost indefinitely. **'Variegata'** has white margins or silver-mottled foliage. It is not as vigorous as the species.

ALTERNATE SPECIES
P. procumbens (Allegheny Spurge, Allegheny Pachysandra) is not as vigorous or hardy as Japanese Spurge. It is attractive in a border as a small clump, rather than as a mass of groundcover.

PROBLEMS & PESTS
Problems with leaf blight, root rot, scale insects and slugs can occur.

Pasque Flower

Pulsatilla

Height: 10–30 cm (4–12") **Spread:** 20–30 cm (8–12")
Flower colour: purple, blue, red, white
Blooms: early to mid-spring **Hardiness:** semi-hardy to tender

*T*his endearing plant is one of the first plants to bloom in spring, the flowers often unfolding from beneath the last of the snow. Plant it near a path where you can pause to admire its beauty while completing spring chores. Once the flowers are gone, the pretty, fluffy seedheads persist to delight gardeners.

PLANTING

Seeding: Sow seed as soon as it is ripe and when soil temperature is about 21° C (70° F).
Planting out: Spring.
Spacing: 20–30 cm (8–12") apart.

GROWING

Pasque Flower grows well in **full sun** or **partial shade**. Soil should be **fertile** and **very well drained**. Poorly drained, wet soil can quickly kill this plant. Pasque Flower resents being disturbed in any way. Plant it while it is very small and don't divide it.

Propagate Pasque Flower by taking root cuttings in early spring. You may have to soak the soil around the plant to loosen it enough to get to the roots. Dig carefully to expose a root, then remove it and replant it. Take a look at the 'Propagation' section in the introduction for more information about starting root cuttings.

TIPS

Pasque Flower can be included in rock gardens, in borders and on gravelly banks. Where it is not hardy, Pasque Flower can be grown in pots or planters and moved to a sheltered spot, perhaps in a corner of the garage, or an enclosed but unheated porch, for the winter. Make sure the pots are moved into the light once the plant begins to show signs of growth.

RECOMMENDED

P. vulgaris (Anemone Pulsatilla) forms a mounded clump of lacy foliage. Flowers in shades of blue, purple or occasionally white are borne in early spring, before the foliage emerges. The seedheads are very fluffy and provide interest when the flowers are gone. **Var. *alba*** has white flowers. **'Rubra'** has bright purple-red flowers.

P. vulgaris var. *alba*

Peony
Paeonia

Height: 60–80 cm (24–32") **Spread:** 60–80 cm (24–32")
Flower colour: white, cream white, yellow, pink, red or purple
Blooms: spring, early summer **Hardiness:** hardy

*P*eonies are often described as one of the 'backbone' plants of the perennial border, plants that provide a good display all season. The beauty of the flowers and their delicate fragrance cast a strong spell over gardeners. Once the fleeting, but magnificent, flower display is done, the foliage remains stellar throughout the growing season. The variety of named cultivars is daunting, but most gardeners find they have favourites once they become more familiar with these perennials.

PLANTING

Seeding: Not recommended. Seeds may take two to three years to germinate and many more years to grow to flowering size.
Planting out: Spring or fall.
Spacing: 60–90 cm (24–36").

GROWING

Peonies prefer **full sun**, but they will tolerate partial shade. The planting site should be well prepared before the plants are introduced. Peonies like **fertile, humus-rich, moist** and **well-drained** soil, to which lots of compost has been added. Division is not required, but it is usually the best way to propagate new plants and should be done in fall.

TIPS

These are wonderful plants that look great in a border when combined with other early-flowering plants. They may be underplanted with bulbs and other plants that will die down by mid-summer, when the emerging foliage of peonies will hide the dying foliage of spring plants.

In the past peonies were used to cure a variety of ailments. They are named after Paion, who was the physician to the Greek gods.

Planting depth is a very important factor in determining whether or not a peony will flower. Tubers planted too shallowly or, more commonly, too deeply will not flower. The buds or eyes on the tuber should be 2.5–5 cm (1–2") below the soil surface.

Cut back the flowers after blooming and remove any blackened leaves to prevent the spread of *Botrytis* blight. Red peonies are more susceptible to disease.

Use wire tomato or peony cages around the plants in early spring to support heavy flowers.

Despite their exotic appearance, peonies are tough and hardy perennials that can even survive winter temperatures of -40° C (-40° F).

RECOMMENDED

Peonies may be listed as cultivars of a certain species or as interspecies hybrids. There are hundreds available.

P. lactiflora (Common Garden Peony, Chinese Peony) forms a clump of red-tinged stems and dark green foliage. It grows up to 75 cm (30") tall, with an equal spread, and bears single, fragrant white or pink flowers with yellow stamens. Some popular hybrid cultivars are **'Dawn Pink'** with single, rose pink flowers, **'Duchess de Nemours'** with fragrant, white, double flowers tinged yellow at the bases of the interior

petals and **'Sara Bernhardt'** with large, double, fragrant pink flowers. These cultivars are often sold as hybrids and not as cultivars of this species.

P. officinalis (Common Peony) forms a clump of slightly hairy stems and deeply lobed foliage. It bears single red or pink flowers with yellow stamens. It grows 60–80 cm (24–32") tall, with an equal spread. Two of the cultivars are **'Alba Plena'** with white, double flowers and **'Rubra Plena'** with red, double flowers.

PROBLEMS & PESTS
Peonies may have trouble with *Verticillium* wilt, ringspot virus, tip blight, stem rot, *Botrytis* blight, leaf blotch, nematodes or Japanese beetles.

Phlox

Phlox

Height: 5–120 cm (2–48") **Spread:** 30–90 cm (12–36")
Flower colour: white, blue, purple or pink
Blooms: late spring, fall **Hardiness:** hardy to semi-hardy

One hardly knows where to start with this variable perennial. Phlox come in many shapes and sizes, ranging from low creepers to bushy border plants with flowering periods falling anywhere between early spring and mid-fall. With shrewd selection you could have phlox plants in different parts of the garden blooming almost all summer.

PLANTING

Seeding: Not recommended.
Planting out: Spring.
Spacing: 30–90 cm (12–36") apart.

GROWING

Moss Phlox prefers to grow in **partial shade**.
Garden Phlox and Wild Sweet William prefer to
grow in **full sun**. All three species like **fertile,
humus-rich, moist, well-drained** soil. Divide in
fall or spring. Creeping Phlox spreads out horizontally as it grows. The stems grow roots where
they touch the ground. These plants are easily
propagated by detaching the rooted stems in
spring or early fall. Do not prune Creeping Phlox
in fall—it is an evergreen and will have next
spring's flowers already forming.

TIPS

Low-growing species are useful in a rock garden
or at the front of a border. Taller species may be
used in the middle of a border where they are
particularly effective if planted in groups.

P. paniculata

*Phlox comes in many
forms from low-growing
creepers to tall, clump-
forming uprights. The
many species can be
found in varied climates
from dry, exposed
mountainsides to moist,
sheltered woodlands.*

P. subulata

P. paniculata

P. paniculata

Garden Phlox requires good air circulation to prevent mildew. Wild Sweet William is more resistant to powdery mildew than Garden Phlox.

RECOMMENDED

P. **'Chatahoochee'** is a low, bushy plant. It grows 15–30 cm (6–12") tall and spreads about 30 cm (12"). It produces lavender-blue flowers with darker purple centres for most of the summer and early fall. This hybrid enjoys a lightly shaded spot in the garden.

P. maculata (Wild Sweet William, Early Phlox) forms an upright clump of hairy stems and narrow leaves that are sometimes spotted with red. It grows 60–90 cm (24–36") tall and spreads 45–60 cm (18–24"). Pink, purple or white flowers are borne in conical clusters in the first half of summer. This species has good resistance to powdery mildew. **'Omega'** bears white flowers with light pink centres. **'Rosalinde'** bears dark pink flowers. Both these cultivars are taller than the species, usually 75 cm (30") or taller.

P. paniculata (Garden Phlox) has many cultivars. They vary greatly in size from 50–120 cm
(20–48") tall with a spread of 60–90 cm (24–36").
There are many colours available, often with
contrasting centres. Garden Phlox blooms in
summer and fall. **'Bright Eyes'** bears light pink
flowers with deeper pink centres. **'David'** bears
white flowers and is resistant to powdery mildew.
'Starfire' bears crimson red flowers.

P. stolonifera (Creeping Phlox) is a low, spreading plant. It grows 10–15 cm (4–6") tall, spreads
about 30 cm (12") and bears flowers in variable
shades of purple in spring. This species tolerates
heavy shade and was formerly a 'Perennial Plant
of the Year.'

P. subulata (Creeping Phlox, Moss Phlox, Moss
Pinks) is very low growing, only 5–15 cm (2–6")
tall, with a spread of 50 cm (20"). It also has cultivars with flowers that bloom in various colours
from late spring to early summer. **'Candy Stripe'**
bears bicoloured pink and white flowers.

PROBLEMS & PESTS
Occasional problems with powdery mildew, stem
canker, rust, leaf spot, leaf miners and caterpillars are possible.

P. paniculata

P. subulata

Pincushion Flower

Scabiosa

Height: 30–60 cm (12–24") **Spread:** 60 cm (24")
Flower colour: purple, blue, white, pink
Blooms: summer **Hardiness:** hardy

One of the first plants I ever grew was Pincushion Flower. The scent of its flowers was most impressive. Breeders have since improved this plant, and it now turns up in many respectable gardens and as a showy flower in florists' arrangements.

PLANTING

Seeding: Direct sow in spring or summer.
Planting out: Spring.
Spacing: 60 cm (24") apart.

GROWING

Pincushion Flower prefers **full sun** but will tolerate partial shade. Soil should be **light, moderately fertile, neutral or alkaline** and **well drained.** Divide in early spring whenever the clumps become overgrown.

TIPS

These plants look best when they are planted in groups in a bed or border. They are also used as cut flowers.

Remove the flowers as they fade to promote a longer flowering period. Cutting flowers at their peak every few days for indoor use will make this maintenance chore more enjoyable.

RECOMMENDED

S. caucasica forms a basal rosette of narrow leaves. Blue or lavender flowers are borne on long stems that grow up to 60 cm (24") tall, with an equal spread. **'Fama'** bears sky blue flowers with silvery-white centres. **'House's Hybrids'** (Isaac House Hybrids) is a group of slightly smaller plants with large, shaggy, blue flowers. **'Miss Wilmont'** bears white flowers.

Several hybrids have been developed from crosses between *S. caucasica* and *S. columbaria*, a smaller species. These hybrids may be listed as cultivars of either species. **'Butterfly Blue'** bears lavender-blue flowers from early summer until frost. **'Pink Mist'** grows about 30 cm (12") tall and bears many pink blooms all season.

PROBLEMS & PESTS

Pincushion Flower or other kinds of *Scabiosa* rarely have any problems. Sometimes aphids can be troublesome.

'Miss Wilmont'

Pinks

Dianthus

Height: 5–45 cm (2–18") **Spread:** 20–60 cm (8–24")
Flower colour: pink, red, white or lilac purple
Blooms: spring, summer **Hardiness:** hardy to semi-hardy

From tiny and delicate to large and robust, this genus contains a wide variety of plants, including Sweet Williams and carnations. The two things most pinks share is their love of well-drained soil and their ruffled petal edges, which appear to have been trimmed with pinking shears, giving them their common name. Many species also have spice-scented flowers.

PLANTING
Seeding: Not recommended. Cultivars do not come true to type from seed.
Planting out: Spring.
Spacing: 25–50 cm (10–20") apart.

GROWING

A location with **full sun** is preferable, but some light shade will be tolerated. A **neutral or alkaline** soil is required. The most important factor in the successful cultivation of pinks is drainage—they hate to stand in water. Mix sand or gravel into their area of the flowerbed to encourage good drainage.

D. plumarius

Pinks may be difficult to propagate by division. It is often easier to take cuttings in summer, once flowering has finished. Cuttings should be 2.5–8 cm (1–3") long. Strip the lower leaves from the cutting. The cuttings should be kept humid, but be sure to give them some ventilation so that fungal problems do not set in. Frequent division, each year or two, will keep the plants vigorous. Divide plants in early spring.

TIPS

Pinks make excellent plants for rock gardens and rock walls, and for edging flower borders and walkways.

D. plumarius

D. plumarius

The tiny, delicate petals of pinks can be used to decorate cakes. Be sure to remove the white part at the base of the petal before using the petals or they will be bitter.

Deadhead as the flowers fade to prolong blooming. Leave a few flowers in place to go to seed. The plants will self-seed quite easily. Seedlings may differ from the parent plants, often with new and interesting results.

RECOMMENDED

D. x *allwoodii* (Allwood Pinks) forms a compact mound and bears flowers in a wide range of colours. Cultivars generally grow 20–45 cm (8–18") tall, with an equal spread. **'Doris'** bears semi-double, salmon pink flowers with darker pink centres. It is popular as a cut flower. **'Laced Romeo'** bears spice-scented red flowers with cream-margined petals. **'Sweet Wivelsfield'** bears fragrant, two-toned flowers in a variety of colours.

D. *deltoides* (Maiden Pink) grows 15–30 cm (6–12") tall and about 30 cm (12") wide. The plant forms a mat of foliage and flowers in spring. This is a popular species in rock gardens. **'Brilliant'** ('Brilliancy,' 'Brilliance') bears dark red flowers.

D. deltoides

D. gratianopolitamus (Cheddar Pink) usually grows about 15 cm (6") tall but can grow up to 30 cm (12") tall and 45–60 cm (18–24") wide. This plant is long-lived and forms a very dense mat of evergreen, silver-grey foliage with sweet-scented flowers borne in summer. **'Petite'** is an even smaller plant, growing 5–10 cm (2–4") tall, with pink flowers.

D. plumarius (Cottage Pink) is noteworthy for its role in the development of many popular cultivars known as Garden Pinks. They are generally 30–45 cm (12–18") tall and 60 cm (24") wide, although smaller cultivars are available. They all flower in spring and into summer if deadheaded regularly. The flowers can be single, semi-double or fully double and are available in many colours. **'Spring Beauty'** bears double flowers in many colours with more strongly frilled edges than the species. **'Sonata'** bears fragrant double flowers in many colours all summer.

PROBLEMS & PESTS
Providing good drainage and air circulation will keep most fungal problems away. Occasional problems with slugs, blister beetles, sow bugs and grasshoppers are possible.

D. deltoides

The Cheddar Pink is a rare and protected species in Britain. It was discovered in the 18th century by British botanist Samuel Brewer, and it became as locally famous as Cheddar cheese.

D. plumarius

Potentilla
Cinquefoil
Potentilla

Height: 8–90 cm (3–36") **Spread:** 15–60 cm (6–24")
Flower colour: yellow, red, orange, pink or white
Blooms: summer **Hardiness:** semi-hardy

Many gardeners are unfamiliar with these herbaceous relatives of the common shrub, but this perennial has much to offer. Attractive flowers and a relaxed, trailing or mounding habit make this plant ideal for borders, rock gardens and planters. Plants can be difficult to find, but seeds are available from several catalogues. Once you have a few plants growing, you may find friends and neighbours asking you for divisions.

PLANTING

Seeding: Start in containers in early spring. Keep soil moist and temperature at about 21° C (70° F).
Planting out: Spring or fall.
Spacing: 30–60 cm (12–24") apart.

GROWING

Potentilla will grow equally well in **full sun** or **partial shade**—these plants are very drought tolerant but should be protected from hot afternoon sun. Soil should be of **poor to average fertility** and **well drained.** Divide in spring or fall, whenever the centre of the plant begins to thin or die out.

TIPS

Potentilla plants make attractive additions to borders, rock gardens and rock walls. Group taller types close together to support each other. Shear back plants of the cultivar 'Miss Willmott' to keep them neat and compact.

RECOMMENDED

P. atrosanguinea (Himalayan Cinquefoil) forms a large clump of sprawling stems and foliage. It grows 30–90 cm (12–36") tall and spreads about 60 cm (24"). Its leaves have silvery hairs on the undersides. Saucer-shaped flowers in yellow, orange or red are borne from summer to fall.

P. 'Monsieur Rouillard' is a hybrid cultivar. It grows about 45–60 cm (18–24") tall, with an equal spread, and bears bright red double flowers all summer. Seed-grown plants occasionally have yellow flowers.

P. 'Melton Fire' grows about 30 cm (12") tall, spreads 45–60 cm (18–24") and bears large red-and-yellow bicoloured flowers all summer.

P. nepalensis (Nepal Cinquefoil) forms a loose clump of trailing stems. It grows 30–45 cm (12–18") tall, spreads up to 60 cm (24") and bears rose pink flowers from late spring to early summer. **'Miss Willmott'** bears scarlet flowers with darker, contrasting centres.

P. neumanniana is mat-forming, grows about 10 cm (4") tall and spreads 30 cm (12"). Bright yellow flowers are borne in spring and through summer. **'Nana'** is even more compact. It grows 8 cm (3") tall and spreads 15 cm (6"). The flowers are yellow.

PROBLEMS & PESTS

Occasional problems with mildew, leaf blister, rust and fungal leaf spot can usually be prevented with good drainage.

Primrose
Primula

Height: 15–60 cm (6–24") **Spread:** 15–45 cm (6–18")
Flower colour: red, orange, pink, purple, blue, white or yellow
Blooms: spring, early summer **Hardiness:** hardy

*P*rimroses deserve to be used more often in gardens. The rosettes of leaves can be smooth and fleshy or deeply veined and crinkled. The flowers appear before you know it, in early spring. I uncovered some flowering beneath a blanket of snow in my mother's garden in late February. The variety of bright flower colours is almost limitless.

PLANTING

Seeding: Sow ripe seeds directly in garden at any time of year. Start them indoors in early spring or in cold frame in fall or late winter.
Planting out: Spring.
Spacing: 15–45 cm (6–18") apart.

GROWING

Choose a location for these plants with **full sun** or **partial shade**. Soil should be **moderately fertile, humus rich, moist, well drained** and **neutral or slightly acidic**. Pull off yellowing or dried leaves in fall for fresh new growth in spring. Overgrown clumps should be divided after flowering or in early fall.

P. vialii

P. x polyanthus

P. japonica

TIPS

Primroses may be incorporated into many areas of the garden. There are moisture-loving primroses that may be included in a bog garden or grown in a moist spot in the garden. Woodland Primrose grows well in a woodland garden or under the shade of taller shrubs and perennials in a border or rock garden.

The species with flowers on tall stems look excellent when planted in masses, while the species with solitary flowers peeking out from the foliage are interesting when dotted throughout the garden in odd spots.

RECOMMENDED

P. auricula (Auricula Primrose) forms a rosette of smooth, waxy foliage. Large flowers are clustered at the tops of stout stems. The plant grows up to 20 cm (8") tall and spreads 25 cm (10").

The flowers are usually yellow or cream, but there are many cultivars with flowers in many colours.

P. eliator (Oxslip) grows about 30 cm (12") tall and 15 cm (6") wide. The yellow tubular flowers are clustered at the ends of long stems.

P. japonica (Japanese Primrose) grows 30–60 cm (12–24") tall and 30–45 cm (12–18") wide. It will thrive in moist, boggy conditions. It is a candelabra flowering type, meaning that the long flower stem has up to six evenly spaced rings of flowers along its length.

P. x polyanthus (Polyantha Primrose, Polyantha Hybrids) usually grows 20–30 cm (8–12") tall, with about an equal spread. The flowers are clustered at the tops of stems of variable height. It is available in a wide range of solid colours or bicolours.

P. veris (Cowslip Primrose) forms a rosette of deeply veined, crinkled foliage. Small clusters of tubular yellow flowers are borne at the tops of narrow stems. The plant grows about 25 cm (10") tall, with an equal spread. The leaves and flowers are edible and the flowers can be used to make wine.

P. vialii forms a rosette of deeply veined leaves. The flowers are borne in small spikes. The spike has a two-toned appearance as the red buds open to reveal light violet flowers starting with the lowest flowers. It grows 30–60 cm (12–24") tall and spreads about 30 cm (12").

P. vulgaris (English Primrose, Common Primrose) grows 15–20 cm (6–8") tall and 20 cm (8") wide. The flowers are solitary and borne at the ends of short stems that are slightly longer than the leaves.

PROBLEMS & PESTS
Slugs, strawberry root weevils, aphids, rust and leaf spot are possible problems for primrose plants.

Red-Hot Poker
Torch Lily
Kniphofia

Height: 60–180 cm (24–72") **Spread:** about 60 cm (24")
Flower colour: bright red, orange, yellow or cream white
Blooms: early summer to fall **Hardiness:** semi-hardy to tender

Red-hot Poker has been banished from some gardens just because the flowers are too bright! They are ideal plants for gardeners who like to make bold and daring statements with their gardens. For others, the new cultivars and varieties offer more muted shades of yellow and cream white and don't look as though they could brand anyone who wanders too close.

PLANTING

Seeding: Not recommended. Cultivars do not come true to type and seedlings may take three years to reach flowering size.
Planting out: Spring.
Spacing: 60 cm (24") apart.

GROWING

These plants will grow equally well in **full sun** or **partial shade**. Soil should be **fertile, humus rich, sandy** and **moist**. Do not cut back the foliage in fall—it provides winter protection for the plants. Large clumps may be divided in late spring.

TIPS

To encourage the plants to continue flowering for as long as possible, cut the spent flowers off right where the stem meets the plant.

The plants are sensitive to cold weather. Bundle up the leaves in fall and tie them above the centre bud to keep the crown protected over the winter.

RECOMMENDED

K. **'Little Maid'** grows to only 60 cm (24") tall and has salmon-coloured buds opening to white flowers.

K. **'Royal Standard'** is a large plant, sometimes growing over 90 cm (36") tall. Scarlet buds open to bright yellow flowers in late summer.

K. uvaria forms a large clump of long, narrow foliage. It grows 120 cm (48") tall and spreads about half this much. In fall bright red buds open to orange flowers that fade to yellow as they age. **'Nobilis'** is a large cultivar. It grows up to 180 cm (72") tall with long, orange-red flower spikes, borne from mid-summer to fall.

PROBLEMS & PESTS

This plant rarely has any problems but is susceptible to stem or crown rot. Flowers dropping off unopened may be caused by thrips.

Red-hot Poker makes a bold, vertical statement in the middle or back of a border. These plants look best when grouped together.

Rose-Mallow
Hibiscus

Height: 45–240 cm (18–96") **Spread:** 90 cm (36")
Flower colour: white, red or pink **Blooms:** late summer to frost
Hardiness: semi-hardy

*I*t's hard to believe that such a dramatic and exotic-looking plant is so easy to grow. With moist soil and full sun, this plant will take care of itself, freely producing wonderful flowers the size of dinner plates. Give it space and it will make itself at home in an informal border, next to a fence or by a pond. It doesn't spread, so it will never become invasive.

PLANTING
Seeding: Sow seeds in spring. Ensure soil temperature is 13–18° C (55–64° F).
Planting out: Spring.
Spacing: 90 cm (36").

GROWING

Grow Rose-mallow in **full sun**. Soil should be **humus rich, moist** and **well drained**. Deadhead spent flowers to keep the plant tidy. Divide in spring.

TIPS

This is an interesting plant for the back of an informal border or mixed into a pondside planting. The large flowers make very colourful additions to late-summer gardens. They create a bold focal point when in flower.

Prune plants by one-half in June for bushier, more compact plants.

RECOMMENDED

H. moscheutos is a large, vigorous plant with strong stems. It grows 90–240 cm (36–96") tall and spreads about 90 cm (36"). The huge, mid- and late-summer flowers can be up to 30 cm (12") across and come in shades of red, pink and white. **'Blue River II'** grows about 120 cm (48") tall. It bears pure white flowers. **'Disco Belle'** is a small plant that grows 45–60 cm (18–24") tall. It is often grown as an annual, and its flowers can be red, pink or white. **'Southern Belle'** bears red, pink or white flowers on large plants that grow 120–180 cm (48–72") tall.

PROBLEMS & PESTS

Rose-mallow may develop problems with rust, fungal leaf spot, bacterial blight, *Verticillium* wilt, viruses, and stem or root rot. A few possible insect pests are whiteflies, aphids, scale insects, mites and caterpillars.

The moisture-loving Rose-mallow is one of the most exotic-looking plants you can include in a bog-garden or pondside planting.

Russian Sage
Perovskia

Height: 90–120 cm (36–48") **Spread:** 90–120 cm (36–48")
Flower colour: blue, purple **Blooms:** mid-summer to fall
Hardiness: semi-hardy to tender

Russian Sage creates a billowy haze of lavender-blue in the late-summer garden. It cools down the bright yellows and oranges that dominate as summer turns to fall. These large, long-blooming plants are happy in poor soil and should have a place in every sunny garden.

PLANTING
Seeding: Not recommended. Germination can be very erratic.
Planting out: Spring.
Spacing: 90 cm (36") apart.

The airy habit of this plant creates a mist of silver-purple in the garden.

GROWING

Russian Sage prefers a location with **full sun**. Soil should be **poor to moderately fertile** and **well drained.** Russian Sage does not need dividing.

TIPS

The silvery foliage and blue flowers combine well with other plants in the back of a mixed border and soften the appearance of daylilies. Russian Sage may also be used in a natural garden or on a dry bank.

Cut the plant back to 30 cm (12") in fall or early spring to encourage vigorous, bushy growth.

RECOMMENDED

P. atriplicifolia is a loose, upright plant with silvery-white, finely divided foliage. It grows 90–120 cm (36–48") tall, with an equal spread. The small, lavender-blue flowers, borne in late summer and fall, are loosely held on silvery, branched stems. **'Filagran'** has delicate foliage and an upright habit. **'Longin'** is narrow and erect and has more smoothly edged leaves than other cultivars.

P. **'Blue Spire'** is an upright plant with deep blue flowers and feathery leaves.

'Filagran'

'Filagran'

Sandwort

Arenaria

Height: 2.5–20 cm (1–8") **Spread:** 30 cm (12")
Flower colour: white flowers with yellow eyes
Blooms: late spring, early summer **Hardiness:** semi-hardy to hardy

*T*hese very low plants make wonderful, moss-like groundcovers for well-drained areas. In low traffic areas they make great replacements for a traditional lawn. The beautiful, white, spring flowers are surprisingly large for such small plants.

PLANTING
Seeding: Direct sow in fall.
Planting out: Spring or fall.
Spacing: 25 cm (10") apart.

GROWING
Sandworts like to grow in **full sun** or **light shade**.
Soil should be **poor or average, sandy** and **well drained.** Divide in spring or fall, whenever the centre of the plant begins to thin out.

TIPS
Sandworts do well in a rock garden, on a stone wall or between the paving stones of a path.

These plants like to be watered regularly but don't like standing in water. To avoid spending all summer using the hose or watering can, it is best to plant sandworts beneath taller shrubs and to apply a mulch to the soil surface. Sandworts have shallow roots and will not compete with the larger shrubs. Both the mulch and the sandwort plant will protect the roots of the bigger shrub.

RECOMMENDED
A. montana (Mountain Sandwort) forms a low mat of foliage. It grows 2.5–20 cm (1–8") tall and spreads about 30 cm (12"). It bears white flowers in late spring. This species is hardy.

A. verna (Moss Sandwort) has evergreen, moss-like foliage. It works well between stepping stones. **Var. *caespitosa*** (Irish Moss) is 5 cm (2") tall with star-shaped, white flowers.

PROBLEMS & PESTS
Occasional problems with rust or anther smut are possible.

Sandwort forms an attractive mat of foliage that is inviting to bare feet.

Sedum
Stonecrop
Sedum

Height: 5–60 cm (2–24") **Spread:** 30–60 cm (12–24")
Flower colour: yellow, white, red or pink
Blooms: summer, fall **Hardiness:** hardy

What forgiving plants sedums are. I planted 'Autumn Joy' 14 years ago in a steep, dry section of my garden and have since done nothing more to the plants than view them from afar. In return they bloom and bloom. In some sections this sun lover is now under the shade of Alternate Leaf Dogwood, and still it performs. 'Autumn Joy' adds bronzy colour to the late-season garden. 'Mohrchen,' a newer hybrid from Germany, has deep bronze-red foliage all season long. The dwarf forms of sedum form a ground-hugging succulent carpet.

PLANTING

Seeding: Indoors in early spring. Seed sold is often a mix of different species. You might not get what you hoped for or expected, but you can just as easily be pleasantly surprised.

Planting out: Spring.

Spacing: 45 cm (18") apart.

GROWING

Sedums prefer **full sun** but will tolerate partial shade. Soil should be **average, very well drained** and **neutral to alkaline.** Divide in spring, when needed. Prune back 'Autumn Joy' in May by one-half and insert pruned-off parts into soft soil. Cuttings will root quickly. Early-summer pruning of upright species and hybrids will give compact, bushy plants.

'Brilliant'

S. spurium

Low-growing sedums make an excellent groundcover under trees. Their shallow roots survive well in the competition for space and moisture.

TIPS

Low-growing sedums make excellent groundcovers and rock-garden or rock-wall plants. They also edge beds and borders wonderfully. The taller types give a beautiful late-season display in a bed or border.

RECOMMENDED

S. acre (Gold Moss Stonecrop) grows 5 cm (2") high and spreads indefinitely. The small yellow-green flowers are borne in summer.

S. 'Autumn Joy' (Autumn Joy Sedum) is a popular upright hybrid. The flowers open pink or red and later fade to deep bronze over a long period in late summer and fall. The plant forms a clump 60 cm (24") tall, with an equal spread.

S. 'Mohrchen' forms an upright clump of stems. It grows about 60 cm (24") tall, with an equal spread. Bronze-red summer foliage brightens to

'Vera Jameson'

'Brilliant'

ruby red in the fall. Clusters of pink flowers are borne in late summer and fall.

S. spectabile (Showy Stonecrop) is an upright species with pink flowers borne in late summer. It forms a clump 45 cm (18") tall and wide. **'Brilliant'** bears bright pink flowers.

S. spurium (Two-Row Stonecrop) forms a mat about 10 cm (4") tall and 60 cm (24") wide. The flowers are deep pink or white.

S. 'Vera Jameson' is a low, mounding plant with purple-tinged stems and pinkish-purple foliage. It grows up to 30 cm (12") tall and spreads 45 cm (18"). Clusters of dark pink flowers are borne in late summer and fall.

PROBLEMS & PESTS
Slugs, snails and scale insects may cause trouble for these plants.

'Autumn Joy'

Autumn Joy Sedum brings colour to the late season garden, when few flowers are in bloom.

Shasta Daisy
Leucanthemum

Height: 30–90 cm (12–36") **Spread:** about 60 cm (24")
Flower colour: white with yellow centres **Blooms:** early summer to fall
Hardiness: semi-hardy to tender

Shasta Daisy adds a joyous tone to the summer garden. These plants sway gracefully in the wind, and they combine so usefully with the more vertical perennials such as daylilies and delphiniums. Breeding improvements mean Shasta Daisy cultivars of differing heights and periods of bloom are now available.

PLANTING

Seeding: Start seeds indoors or direct sow in garden in spring. Soil temperature at about 21–24° C (70–75° F).
Planting out: Spring.
Spacing: About 60 cm (24") apart.

GROWING

Shasta Daisy grows well in **full sun** and **partial shade**. Soil should be **fertile, moist** and **well drained**. Divide every year or two, in spring, to maintain plant vigour.

TIPS

Use these perennials in the border where they can be grown as single plants or massed in groups.

Flowers can be cut for fresh arrangements.

Pinch or trim plants back in the spring to encourage compact, bushy growth.

RECOMMENDED

L. **'Marconi'** has large semi-double or double flowers. It prefers partial shade, with protection from the hot afternoon sun.

L. x *superbum* forms a large clump of dark green leaves and stems. It bears white daisy-like flowers with yellow centres all summer, often until the first frost. **'Alaska'** bears large flowers. It is hardier than the species.

PROBLEMS & PESTS

Occasional problems with aphids, leaf spot and leaf miners are possible.

Snow-in-Summer

Cerastium

Height: 5–20 cm (2–8") **Spread:** indefinite
Flower colour: white **Blooms:** late spring, early summer
Hardiness: hardy

Snow-in-summer is a real performer in poor soil and parched places in the garden. On a dry slope, where other plants wither, Snow-in-summer rambles with ease. This plant can be a bully, though, especially in rich soils, overwhelming less vigorous plants with ease.

PLANTING

Seeding: Start seeds early indoors or sow directly in garden for flowers in first year.
Planting out: Spring.
Spacing: 30–45 cm (12–18") apart.

GROWING

Grow Snow-in-summer in **full sun** or **partial shade**. This plant will grow in any type of **well-drained** soil but may develop root rot in wet soil. The richer the soil, the more invasive Snow-in-summer becomes, but it will do well in poor soil. Snow-in-summer tends to die out in the middle as it grows, so dividing it every two years will ensure that it maintains even coverage.

TIPS

Snow-in-summer is well suited to sunny, hot locations. It may be used under taller plants, as a groundcover, along border edges and to prevent erosion on sloping banks. It is attractive on a rock wall but might overwhelm less vigorous plants.

Cutting the plant back after it has finished flowering and again later in summer will help keep growth in check and prevent the plant from thinning out excessively in the centre. It can spread up to 90 cm (36") in a single year.

RECOMMENDED

C. tomentosum forms a low mat of silvery-grey foliage. It grows 5–15 cm (2–6") tall and spreads 30 cm (12") or more. This plant bears white flowers in late spring. **'Silver Carpet'** is a more compact cultivar. **Var. *compactae*** is a shrubbier variety that spreads less.

Soapwort
Saponaria

Height: 8–60 cm (3–24") **Spread:** 45 cm (18"), or more
Flower colour: pink, white, red **Blooms:** spring, summer, fall
Hardiness: hardy

Soapworts are very reliable ground-hugging perennials that put out a carpet of pink flowers. They do so well in lean soil, they can actually become invasive. An upscale version of this plant has recently become available—'Bressingham' is an alpine variety perfect for rock gardens.

Saponin-rich plants such as Saponaria officinalis *were used for cleaning purposes before commercially produced soap became available.*

PLANTING

Seeding: Start seeds in the early spring. Keep the planted seeds in a cool dark place, about 15–18° C (60–65° F), until they germinate. Move into a lighted room as soon as germination begins.
Planting out: Spring.
Spacing: 45 cm (18") apart.

GROWING

Soapworts grow best in **full sun**. Soil should be of **average fertility, neutral to alkaline** and **well drained**. Poor soils are tolerated. Divide in spring every few years to maintain vigour and control spread.

TIPS

Use soapworts in borders, rock gardens and on rock walls. Soapworts can overwhelm less vigorous plants. Cut Rock Soapwort back after flowering to keep it neat and compact.

RECOMMENDED

S. 'Bressingham' grows up to 8 cm (3") tall and spreads about 30 cm (12"). Its green foliage is topped with bright pink flowers in spring. This alpine type works well in the rock garden.

S. ocymoides (Rock Soapwort) forms a low, spreading mound. It grows 10–15 cm (4–6") tall and spreads about 45 cm (18"). The plant is completely covered in bright pink flowers in late spring and continues to flower sporadically all summer. **'Alba'** has white flowers. **'Rubra Compacta'** is very low growing, with dark pink flowers.

S. officinalis (Soapwort, Bouncing Bet) is an upright plant. It grows up to 60 cm (24") tall and spreads about 45 cm (18"). This plant is aggressive and can quickly spread even farther with good growing conditions. Pink, white or red flowers are borne from summer to fall. Cultivars are not as invasive as the species. **'Rosea Plena'** bears fragrant, pink, double flowers in early summer.

Speedwell
Veronica
Veronica

Height: 15–60 cm (6–24") **Spread:** 40–45 cm (16–18")
Flower colour: white, pink, purple or blue
Blooms: summer **Hardiness:** hardy

When I first came under the spell of perennial gardening I remember conducting a sweeping search for *Veronica* 'Crater Lake Blue.' It sounded like a cross between Paul Newman's eyes and 'Heavenly Blue' morning glory. I never found it and settled for a speedwell of unknown parentage that added a respectable sky blue to the garden. Many speedwells are lax in their habit but beloved for their flowers; others in the creeping category skim the ground and are not prone to spineless behaviour. I like Spike Speedwell planted with billowy hardy geraniums—a good yin and yang.

PLANTING

Seeding: Not recommended. Seedlings do not always come true to type. Seeds germinate quickly if started indoors in early spring.
Planting out: Spring.
Spacing: 45 cm (18") apart.

GROWING

Speedwells prefer **full sun,** but they will tolerate partial shade. Soil should be of **average fertility, moist** and **well drained.** Divide in fall or spring every three or five years.

TIPS

Plant Spike Speedwell in masses in a bed or border. Prostrate Speedwell is useful in a rock garden or at the front of a border. Deadhead to encourage longer blooming. For tidier plants, shear back tall types to 15 cm (6") in June.

Subsp. *incana*

RECOMMENDED

V. prostrata (Prostrate Speedwell) is a low-growing, spreading plant. It grows 15 cm (6") tall and spreads 40 cm (16"). Its flowers may be blue or occasionally pink. Many cultivars are available.

V. spicata (Spike Speedwell) is a low, mounding plant with stems that flop over when they get too tall. It grows 30–60 cm (12–24") tall and spreads 45 cm (18"). It bears spikes of blue flowers in summer. Many cultivars of different colours are available. **Subsp. *incana*** has soft, hairy, silvery-green leaves and deep purple-blue flowers. **'Red Fox'** has dark red-pink flowers.

PROBLEMS & PESTS

Problems with scale insects are possible, as are fungal problems such as downy mildew, powdery mildew, rust, leaf smut and root rot.

'Red Fox'

Sweet Woodruff

Galium

Height: 30–45 cm (12–18") **Spread:** indefinite
Flower colour: white **Blooms:** late spring to mid-summer
Hardiness: semi-hardy

Sweet Woodruff is a groundcover of abundant good qualities. The foliage has a subtle, endearing fragrance like new-mown hay. In May the plant produces a froth of white flowers. It seems to grow on command—snitch a piece from a planting under a shrub and tuck it in near thinning perennials, and it easily skips along and fills in the bald spot. The star-shaped leaves marry smoothly with so many other foliage shapes, such as the leaves of Canada Wild Ginger and hostas. This is a first-rate groundcover for shady to partly sunny areas.

PLANTING
Seeding: Not recommended.
Planting out: Spring or fall.
Spacing: 30 cm (12") apart.

GROWING
This plant prefers **partial shade**. It will grow well, but will not bloom well, in full shade. Soil should be **humus rich** and **evenly moist**. Divide plants in spring or fall.

TIPS
Sweet Woodruff is a perfect woodland ground-cover. It forms a beautiful green carpet and loves the same conditions in which azaleas and rhododendrons thrive. Shear back after blooming to encourage plants to fill in with foliage and crowd out weeds.

RECOMMENDED
G. odoratum is a low, spreading groundcover. Clusters of star-shaped, white flowers are borne in late spring.

PROBLEMS & PESTS
Sweet Woodruff may have problems with mildew, rust and fungal leaf spot.

The dried leaves were once used to scent doorways and freshen stale rooms.

The wiry, creeping habit of Sweet Woodruff makes it an excellent groundcover; it is particularly effective under trees. The white flowers seem to glow at dusk in late spring.

Tansy
Tanacetum

Height: 20–120 cm (8–48") **Spread:** 25–90 cm (12–36")
Flower colour: yellow-centered, white, pink, purple, yellow or red
Blooms: summer **Hardiness:** hardy to semi-hardy

*T*ansies are very dependable members of the daisy family. These hard-working flowers will bloom over a long period and will stay orderly after being pinched back in May or June. Included in this flower group are Feverfew, useful to many migraine sufferers, and Pyrethrum, which has insecticidal attributes.

PLANTING

Seeding: Start seed in early spring. Soil temperature should be 10–13°C (50–55° F).
Planting out: Spring.
Spacing: 30–90 cm (12–36") apart.

GROWING

Tansies grow best in **full sun**. Any **well-drained** soil is suitable. Very fertile soil may encourage invasive growth. Deadheading will prolong the blooming period. Divide in spring as needed to control spread and maintain plant vigour.

TIPS

Use tansies in borders, rock gardens, wildflower gardens, cottage gardens and meadow gardens. Most of these species are quite civilized, but *T. vulgare* can become quite invasive. To control invasiveness, grow the less-invasive cultivar or grow the species in planters and remove the flowers before the seeds ripen.

RECOMMENDED

T. argenteum forms a low mat of finely divided silvery-grey foliage. It grows 20–30 cm (8–12") tall, spreads 25–45 cm (12–18") and bears daisy-like white flowers.

T. coccineum (Painted Daisy, Pyrethrum) is an erect, bushy plant, growing 45–90 cm (18–36") tall and spreading 30–45 cm (12–18"). The main flush of white, pink, purple or red, yellow-centered flowers occurs in early summer, but some flowering will continue until fall. **'Brenda'** has red or magenta flowers. **'James Kelway'** bears scarlet red flowers.

T. vulgare

T. parthenium (Feverfew) is a bushy plant with fern-like foliage. It grows 30–90 cm (12–36") tall, spreads 30–60 cm (12–24") and bears clusters of small daisy-like flowers. **'Gold Ball'** forms a compact plant bearing yellow double flowers. **'Snowball'** bears double white flowers.

T. vulgare (Tansy, Golden Buttons) forms a large, erect, wide-spreading mound. It grows 60–120 cm (24–48") tall, spreads 45–90 cm (18–36") and bears clusters of bright yellow button-like flowers mid-summer to fall. **'Crispum'** (Curly Tansy) is a compact plant with crinkled, lacy foliage. It is less invasive than the species.

PROBLEMS & PESTS

Tansies are generally pest free, but keep an eye open for aphids.

T. parthenium

Thrift
Sea Pink
Armeria

Height: 20–60 cm (8–24") **Spread:** 30–60 cm (12–24")
Flower colour: pink or white **Blooms:** late spring, early summer
Hardiness: semi-hardy

Old-fashioned and unassuming, the fresh, springtime blooms of Thrift are a comforting sight. It is commonly seen in old, established rock gardens in vintage neighbourhoods. It seems that the breeders have been busy with this plant because I have seen new species and varieties, including one with steel blue foliage. This dependable plant grows in poor conditions and doesn't mind if salt from winter roads has dissolved into the soil.

PLANTING
Seeding: Start seeds in spring or fall. Soak for a few hours before planting.
Planting out: Spring.
Spacing: 25 cm (10") apart.

GROWING
Thrift requires **full sun**. Soil should be **poor or moderate** and **well drained**. Thrift is very drought tolerant. Divide in spring or fall.

TIPS
This is a useful plant in rock gardens or at the front of a border.

If your Thrift plant seems to be dying out in the middle of the clump, then try cutting it back hard. New shoots should fill in quickly.

RECOMMENDED
*A. **maritima*** forms a clump of grassy foliage. Ball-like clusters of white, pink or purple flowers are borne at the ends of long stems in late spring and early summer. The plant grows up to 20 cm (8") tall and spreads about 30 cm (12"). **'Alba'** has white flowers.

A. **'Bees'** is a group of larger hybrids that grow 45–60 cm (18–24") tall, with an equal spread. The large white, pink or red flowers are borne in late spring and summer.

PROBLEMS & PESTS
Problems are rare with this durable plant. It may occasionally get rust or be attacked by aphids.

Attract bees and butterflies to your garden with clumps of Thrift.

Thyme
Thymus

Height: 5–45 cm (2–18") **Spread:** 10–40 cm (4–16")
Flower colour: purple, pink or white **Blooms:** late spring, early summer
Hardiness: semi-hardy

Much fun can be had working different varieties of thyme into the garden. There doesn't seem to be a homely one in the bunch. 'Elfin' is so tiny it is spellbinding, and lemon thymes fill the air with citrus scent. I remember vividly a front yard that consisted of Mother of Thyme, violets and Mugo Pine. It was a vision of gentle mounds carpeted in green.

PLANTING

Seeding: Many popular hybrids, particularly the ones with variegated leaves, cannot be grown from seed. Common Thyme and Mother of Thyme are good choices for starting from seed. Start indoors in early spring.
Planting out: Spring.
Spacing: 40–50 cm (16–20").

GROWING

Thymes prefer **full sun**. Soil should be **average** or **poor** and **very well drained**; it helps to have leaf mould worked into it. It is easy to propagate the cultivars that cannot be started from seed. As the plant grows outwards, the branches touch the ground and send out new roots. These rooted stems may be removed and grown in pots to be planted out the following spring. Unrooted stem cuttings may be taken in early spring, before flowering. Divide plants in spring.

'Golden King'

This large genus has species throughout the world that were used in various ways in several cultures. Ancient Egyptians used it in embalming; the Greeks added it to baths and the Romans purified their rooms with it.

T. serpyllum

T. vulgaris

'Golden King'

TIPS

Thymes are useful plants to include in the front of borders, between or beside paving stones and on rock gardens and rock walls.

Once the plants have finished flowering, it is a good idea to shear them back by about half. This encourages new growth and prevents the plants from becoming too woody.

RECOMMENDED

T. x *citriodorus* (Lemon-Scented Thyme) forms a mound 30 cm (12") tall and 10" (25 cm) wide. The foliage does smell of lemon, and the flowers are pale pink. The cultivars are more ornamental. **'Argenteus'** has silver-edged leaves. **'Aureus'** has yellow-gold variegated leaves. **'Golden King'** has yellow-margined leaves.

T. serpyllum (Mother of Thyme, Wild Thyme) is a popular low-growing species. It usually grows about 13 cm (5") tall and spreads 30 cm (12") or more. The flowers are purple. There are many cultivars available. **'Elfin'** forms tiny, dense mounds of foliage. It grows up to 5–8 cm (2–3") tall and

spreads 10 cm (4"). It rarely flowers. **'Minimus'** grows 5 cm (2") high and 10 cm (4") wide. **'Snowdrift'** has white flowers.

T. vulgaris (Common Thyme) forms a bushy mound of dark green leaves. The flowers may be purple, pink or white. It usually grows about 30–45 cm (12–18") tall and spreads about 40 cm (16"). **'Silver Posie'** is a good cultivar with pale pink flowers and silver-edged leaves.

PROBLEMS & PESTS
Thyme plants rarely have any problems. Seedlings may suffer from damping off and plants may get grey mould or root rot. Good circulation and adequate drainage are good ways to avoid these problems.

In the Middle Ages, it was believed that drinking a thyme infusion would enable one to see fairies.

T. serpyllum

Vinca
Periwinkle
Vinca

Height: 10–20 cm (4–8") **Spread:** indefinite
Flower colour: blue-purple; sometimes pale blue, reddish purple or white
Blooms: mid-spring to fall **Hardiness:** hardy to semi-hardy

Vinca is a very dependable ground-cover for partial to full shade. With glossy, deep green leaves and periwinkle blue flowers, it has an attractive presence in the garden. Because it is not a terribly dense groundcover, it can be underplanted with some of the smaller spring bulbs. Snowdrops, muscari and scilla will poke up in the spring, flower, and then have their fading foliage disguised by the Vinca.

PLANTING
Seeding: Not recommended.
Planting out: Spring or fall.
Spacing: 60–90 cm (24–36") apart.

GROWING
Grow Vinca in **partial to full shade**. It will grow in **any type of soil** as long as it is not too dry. The plants will turn yellow if the soil is too dry or the sun too hot. Divide Vinca in early spring or mid- to late fall or whenever it is becoming overgrown. One plant can cover almost any size of area.

TIPS
Vinca is a useful and attractive groundcover in a shrub border, under trees or on a shady bank, and it prevents soil erosion. Vinca is shallow-rooted and able to out-compete weeds but won't interfere with deeper-rooted shrubs.

If Vinca begins to outgrow its space it may be sheared back hard in early spring. The sheared-off ends may have rooted along the stems. These rooted cuttings may be potted up and given away as gifts or may be introduced to new areas of the garden.

RECOMMENDED
V. minor (Lesser Periwinkle) forms a low, loose mat of trailing stems. Purple or blue flowers are borne in a flush in spring and sporadically all summer. **'Alba'** bears white flowers. **'Atropurpurea'** bears reddish-purple flowers.

The Romans used the long, trailing stems of Vinca to make wreaths. This use of the plant may have given it the name Vinca, which is derived from the Latin word vincire, *meaning 'to bind.'*

The glossy green foliage of Vinca remains attractive and cooling in the heat of summer, long after the flowering has finished.

Violet

Viola

Height: 8–20 cm (3–8") **Spread:** 30–40 cm (12–16")
Flower colour: purple, blue, white, yellow or orange
Blooms: spring and early summer, sometimes again in fall
Hardiness: hardy to semi-hardy

Because they are so easy to grow, it is convenient to snub violets. But these plants have some fine qualities, including the ability to grow in shade or sun, smother weeds and produce flowers that are fragrant and adorable. *Viola sororia* 'Freckles' is a speckled beauty.

PLANTING
Seeding: Indoors in spring.
Planting out: Spring.
Spacing: 30 cm (12") apart.

GROWING
Violets will grow equally well in **full sun** or **partial shade**. Soil should be **fertile, humus rich, moist** and **well drained**. Violets self-seed freely and you may find them cropping up here and there in unlikely places in the garden. Cultivars may not set seed. Divide in spring or fall.

TIPS
Violets are good for rock gardens, walls and the front of a border but can be invasive.

RECOMMENDED
V. cornuta (Horned Violet) is a low-growing, wide-spreading plant. It grows 15 cm (6") tall and 40 cm (16") wide. Cultivars are available in all colours.

V. labrodorica (Labrador Violet) spreads indefinitely with small clumps of foliage, growing about 8 cm (3") tall. Purple flowers are produced in spring and summer.

V. odorata (Sweet Violet) is a sweet-scented plant that grows 20 cm (8") tall and 30 cm (12") wide. The flowers are blue or white.

V. riviniana (Dog Violet, Wood Violet) forms small tufty rosettes of foliage. It grows up to 20 cm (8") tall and spreads up to 40 cm (16") wide. Light violet flowers are borne in late spring and early summer.

V. sororia (Woolly Blue Violet) forms a small clump of foliage with fuzzy undersides. It grows 10 cm (4") tall and spreads 20 cm (8"). Its flowers are purple or white with purple dots and streaks, borne in spring and summer. 'Freckles' has white flowers that are speckled with light purple dots.

In Greek mythology, the violet was the flower of Aphrodite, the goddess of love, and of her son, Priapus, the god of gardens. The Greeks named the violet the symbol of Athens.

Wall Rockcress
Rock Cress
Arabis

Height: 5–30 cm (2–12") **Spread:** 30–45 cm (12–18")
Flower colour: white, pink **Blooms:** mid- to late spring
Hardiness: hardy to semi-hardy

Several years ago I was introduced to the 'Anything but Green Plant Society.' Followers of this sect will use only plants with variegated leaves. They are the types to swoon over Variegated Rock Cress. Variegated Rock Cress has shiny dark green foliage edged in white. The flowers, also white, may take a back seat to the carpet of two-toned leaves.

PLANTING

Seeding: Start in container in early spring. Seeds require light for germination.
Planting out: Any time during growing season.
Spacing: 30 cm (12") apart.

GROWING

Wall Rockcress prefers to grow in **full sun**. Soil should be **average or poor** and **well drained**. It should have plenty of **lime** mixed in because it needs an alkaline soil. This plant will do best in a climate that doesn't have extremely hot summer weather. Stem cuttings, taken from the new growth, may be started in summer. Divide in early fall every two or three years.

TIPS

Use Wall Rockcress in a rock garden, a border or on a rock wall. It may also be used as a groundcover on an exposed slope or as a companion plant with small bulbs.

Cut the plant back after flowering to keep it neat and compact. Don't plant Wall Rockcress where it may overwhelm plants that are slower growing.

RECOMMENDED

A. caucasica forms a low mound of small rosettes of foliage. White flowers are borne in early spring. **'Snow Cap'** ('Schneehaube') produces abundant white flowers. **'Compinkie'** has pink flowers.

A. procurrens (*A. ferdinandi-coburgi*) forms a low mat of foliage. It bears small white flowers in spring and early summer. This species is more shade tolerant than *A. caucasica*. **'Variegata'** (Variegated Rock Cress) has white-edged foliage.

PROBLEMS & PESTS

White rust, downy mildew and rust are possible. Aphids are occasionally a problem along with *Arabis* midge, which causes deformed shoots that should be removed and destroyed.

Arabis *looks quite a lot like* Aubrieta. *They are both commonly known as rock cress, so make sure you write down the botanical name of the plant you want before taking a trip to the garden centre to buy it.*

Wild Ginger
Asarum

Height: 8–15 cm (3–6") **Spread:** 30 cm (12"), or wider
Flower colour: burgundy and green, inconspicuous; foliage plant
Blooms: early summer **Hardiness:** hardy to semi-hardy

Shade-loving wild ginger plants deserve to be used more often. Their heart-shaped leaves combine well with ferns, Sweet Woodruff or corydalis, creating contrasts in texture. When the leaves first emerge in the spring, they are a beguiling fuzzy grey before they attain their mature shape. A few cut leaves look good tucked into simple flower arrangements. European Wild Ginger has a small, glossy and rounded leaf, with very pretty, reflective qualities.

PLANTING
Seeding: Not recommended.
Planting out: Spring or fall.
Spacing: 30 cm (12") apart.

GROWING
Wild gingers need to be in the **shade** or **partial shade**. Soil should be **moist** and **humus rich**. Wild gingers will tolerate drought for a while in good shade, but prolonged drought will eventually cause the plants to wilt and die back. All *Asarum* species prefer to grow in acid soils, but *A. canadense* will tolerate alkaline conditions. Division is unlikely to be necessary, except to propagate more plants.

TIPS
Use wild gingers in a shady rock garden, border or woodland garden.

The thick, fleshy rhizomes grow along the soil or just under it, and pairs of leaves grow up from the rhizomes. Cuttings can be made by cutting off the sections of rhizome with leaves growing from them and planting each section separately. When taking cuttings, you must be careful not to damage the tiny thread-like roots that grow from the stem below the point where the leaves grow up.

Wild ginger rhizomes have a distinctive ginger scent; though they are not related to the ginger commonly used in cooking, they may be used as a flavouring in many dishes.

A. canadense

RECOMMENDED
A. canadense (Canada Wild Ginger) is native to eastern North America. The heart-shaped leaves are slightly hairy. The roots of this wild ginger can be used in place of true ginger in recipes.

A. europaeum (European Wild Ginger) is a European native. The leaves of this plant are very glossy and it is the quickest species to spread over an area. This species is not as heat tolerant as Canada Wild Ginger.

Yarrow

Achillea

Height: 30–120 cm (12–48") **Spread:** 40–60 cm (16–24")
Flower colour: white, yellow, red, orange or pink
Blooms: mid-summer to early fall **Hardiness:** hardy

Yarrows are informal, tough plants that have a fantastic colour range. There's nothing subtle about 'Coronation Gold' with its egg yolk yellow blooms. Put it next to 'Purple Rain' salvia and it looks like something out of a psychedelic Easter basket. 'Summer Pastels,' on the other hand, is a blend of soft and subtle shades that mix well with ornamental grasses.

PLANTING
Seeding: Direct sow in spring. Don't cover the seeds; they need light to germinate.
Planting out: Spring.
Spacing: 30–60 cm (12–24").

GROWING
Grow yarrows in **full sun**. Yarrows will do well in an **average to sandy soil** or any soil that is **well drained**. These plants are tolerant of drought and poor soil but will not do well in a heavy, wet soil and are not tolerant of high humidity. Remove the flowerheads once they begin to fade. Yarrows will flower more profusely and longer if they are deadheaded. Divide every four or five years, in spring or fall.

'Summer Pastels'

'Cerise Queen'

The ancient Druids used yarrow to divine seasonal weather, and the ancient Chinese used it to foretell the future.

A. millefolium

TIPS

Yarrows are very informal plants. They look best when grown in a natural-looking garden. Cottage gardens and wildflower gardens are perfect places to grow yarrows. These plants thrive in hot, dry locations where nothing else will grow.

Yarrow plants make excellent groundcovers, despite being quite tall. The plants send up shoots and flowers from a low basal point and may be mowed periodically without excessive damage to the plant. Mower blades should be kept quite high, i.e., no lower than 10 cm (4"). Keep in mind that you are mowing off the flowerheads. Do not mow more often than once a month, or you will have short yarrow but no flowers!

Yarrows are used in fresh or dried arrangements. Pick flowers only after pollen is visible on the flowers or they will die very quickly.

RECOMMENDED

A. filipendulina has yellow flowers and grows up to 120 cm (48") tall. It has been used in the development of several hybrids. There are also several cultivars of varied heights and flowers in various shades of yellow.

A. filipendulina

A. millefolium (Common Yarrow) is 30–90 cm (12–36") tall and has white flowers. The species is almost never grown in favour of the many cultivars that have been developed. **'Cerise Queen'** has pinkish-red flowers. **'Summer Pastels'** has flowers of many colours. This is the most heat- and drought-tolerant cultivar and has fade-resistant flowers.

PROBLEMS & PESTS

Rare problems with powdery mildew and stem rot are possible.

Yarrow has blood coagulant properties that were recognized by the ancient Greeks. Achillea is named after the legend of Achilles because during the battle of Troy he treated the wounds of his warriors with this herb.

A. millefolium

Quick Reference Chart

HEIGHT LEGEND: Low: < 30 cm (12")-•-Medium: 30–60 cm (12–24")-•-Tall: > 60 cm (24")

SPECIES by Common Name	White	Pink	Red	Orange	Yellow	Blue	Purple	Foliage	Spring	Summer	Fall	Low	Medium	Tall
Ajuga	*	*				*	*	*	*	*		*		
Anemone	*	*			*	*			*	*	*	*	*	*
Artemisia	*				*			*		*		*	*	*
Aster	*	*	*			*	*			*	*	*	*	*
Astilbe	*	*	*				*			*		*	*	*
Balloon Flower	*	*				*				*				*
Basket-of-gold					*				*			*	*	
Beard Tongue	*	*	*		*		*		*	*	*		*	*
Bellflower	*	*				*	*		*	*		*	*	*
Bergamot	*	*	*				*			*				*
Bergenia	*	*	*			*	*		*				*	
Black-eyed Susan			*	*	*					*	*	*	*	
Blazing Star	*						*			*		*	*	
Bleeding Heart	*	*	*				*		*	*		*	*	
Butterfly Weed			*	*	*					*	*	*	*	
Candytuft	*								*			*		
Cardinal Flower	*	*	*		*	*				*	*			*
Catmint	*	*				*	*		*	*			*	*
Christmas Rose	*	*			*		*		*			*	*	
Columbine	*	*	*		*	*	*		*	*			*	*
Coneflower	*	*					*			*				*
Coral Bells	*	*	*		*		*	*	*	*			*	*
Coreopsis		*		*	*					*			*	*
Corydalis						*	*		*	*	*	*	*	
Cupid's Dart	*					*	*			*	*	*	*	
Daylily		*	*	*	*		*			*	*		*	*
Dead Nettle	*	*			*		*	*	*	*		*	*	
Delphinium	*	*				*	*		*	*				*
Doronicum					*				*	*		*	*	

Quick Reference Chart

Hardy	Semi-hardy	Tender	Sun	Part Shade	Light Shade	Shade	Moist	Well Drained	Dry	Fertile	Average	Poor	Page Number	SPECIES by Common Name
HARDINESS			LIGHT				SOIL CONDITIONS							
*			*	*	*	*		*		*	*	*	68	Ajuga
*	*			*	*		*		*	*	*		72	Anemone
*	*		*					*		*	*		76	Artemisia
*	*		*	*			*	*		*			80	Aster
*				*	*		*	*		*			84	Astilbe
*			*	*			*	*		*	*		88	Balloon Flower
*			*					*	*		*	*	90	Basket-of-gold
*			*	*				*		*	*		94	Beard Tongue
*			*	*	*			*		*	*		98	Bellflower
*			*	*	*	*	*				*		102	Bergamot
*			*	*				*		*	*		106	Bergenia
*			*	*				*		*			110	Black-eyed Susan
*			*				*	*		*			112	Blazing Star
*					*		*			*			114	Bleeding Heart
*			*					*		*	*		118	Butterfly Weed
	*		*				*	*			*	*	120	Candytuft
*	*		*	*	*		*			*			122	Cardinal Flower
*	*		*	*				*		*			126	Catmint
	*	*			*		*	*		*			130	Christmas Rose
*			*	*			*	*		*			132	Columbine
*			*		*			*		*	*		136	Coneflower
*				*	*		*	*		*	*		140	Coral Bells
*	*		*					*		*			144	Coreopsis
	*	*	*	*	*			*		*	*		148	Corydalis
*			*	*				*		*			150	Cupid's Dart
*			*	*	*	*	*	*		*			152	Daylily
*	*			*	*		*	*		*			156	Dead Nettle
*			*				*	*		*			160	Delphinium
*			*	*	*		*				*	*	164	Doronicum

Quick Reference Chart

HEIGHT LEGEND: Low: < 30 cm (12")-•-Medium: 30–60 cm (12–24")-•-Tall: > 60 cm (24")

SPECIES by Common Name	White	Pink	Red	Orange	Yellow	Blue	Purple	Foliage	Spring	Summer	Fall	Low	Medium	Tall
English Daisy	*	*	*		*				*	*		*		
Euphorbia					*			*	*	*			*	
Evening Primrose	*	*			*				*	*		*	*	*
False Dragonhead	*	*					*			*	*		*	*
False Rockcress	*	*					*		*	*		*		
False Solomon's Seal	*							*	*					*
Foamflower	*	*						*	*					
Foxglove	*	*	*		*		*			*				*
Geum		*	*	*	*					*			*	
Goat's Beard	*									*				*
Goutweed	*							*		*		*	*	
Hardy Geranium	*	*	*			*	*			*		*	*	*
Hens and Chicks	*		*		*		*	*		*		*		
Hollyhock	*	*	*		*		*			*				*
Hosta	*					*	*	*		*	*	*	*	*
Iris	*	*	*		*	*	*		*	*		*	*	*
Jacob's Ladder	*					*	*		*	*		*	*	*
Lady's Mantle					*			*		*	*	*	*	
Lamb's Ears		*					*	*		*		*	*	
Ligularia				*	*			*		*	*			*
Lily-of-the-valley	*	*						*	*			*		
Lungwort	*	*	*			*		*	*			*	*	
Lupine	*	*	*	*	*	*	*			*			*	*
Lychnis	*	*	*							*				*
Mallow	*	*				*	*			*	*	*	*	*
Marguerite Daisy	*				*				*	*				*
Meadow Rue	*	*			*		*		*	*				*
Meadowsweet	*	*							*	*				*
Monkshood	*					*	*			*				*

Quick Reference Chart

Hardy	Semi-hardy	Tender	Sun	Part Shade	Light Shade	Shade	Moist	Well Drained	Dry	Fertile	Average	Poor	Page Number	SPECIES by Common Name
	*		*	*	*		*			*	*		166	English Daisy
*			*		*		*	*	*		*		168	Euphorbia
*			*					*			*	*	170	Evening Primrose
*			*	*	*		*			*	*		172	False Dragonhead
*	*		*	*				*			*		174	False Rockcress
*					*	*	*				*		178	False Solomon's Seal
*				*	*	*	*			*	*	*	180	Foamflower
	*			*	*		*			*			182	Foxglove
	*		*				*	*		*			186	Geum
*				*	*	*	*			*			188	Goat's Beard
*			*	*	*	*		*	*			*	192	Goutweed
*				*	*			*			*		194	Hardy Geranium
*			*	*				*	*		*	*	198	Hens and Chicks
*			*	*						*	*		200	Hollyhock
*				*	*		*	*		*			204	Hosta
*	*		*		*		*	*		*	*		208	Iris
*			*	*			*	*		*			212	Jacob's Ladder
*	*			*	*		*	*		*			214	Lady's Mantle
*	*		*					*	*		*	*	218	Lamb's Ears
	*		*	*	*		*				*		220	Ligularia
*			*	*	*	*	*	*	*	*	*	*	224	Lily-of-the-valley
*	*			*	*	*	*	*		*			228	Lungwort
*	*			*	*			*		*	*		232	Lupine
*	*		*	*				*	*		*		236	Lychnis
	*		*	*			*	*	*		*		238	Mallow
*			*					*	*		*		242	Marguerite Daisy
*	*			*	*		*	*		*	*		244	Meadow Rue
*				*	*		*			*			248	Meadowsweet
*	*				*		*			*			252	Monkshood

Quick Reference Chart

HEIGHT LEGEND: Low: < 30 cm (12")-•-Medium: 30–60 cm (12–24")-•-Tall: > 60 cm (24")

SPECIES by Common Name	White	Pink	Red	Orange	Yellow	Blue	Purple	Foliage	Spring	Summer	Fall	Low	Medium	Tall
Mullein	*			*	*					*				*
Oriental Poppy	*	*	*	*					*	*			*	*
Pachysandra	*							*	*			*		
Pasque Flower	*		*			*	*		*			*		
Peony	*	*	*		*		*	*	*	*				*
Phlox	*	*				*	*		*		*	*		*
Pincushion Flower	*	*				*	*			*			*	*
Pinks	*	*	*				*		*	*		*	*	
Potentilla	*	*	*	*	*					*		*	*	*
Primrose	*	*	*	*	*	*	*		*	*		*	*	
Red-hot Poker	*		*	*	*					*	*			*
Rose-mallow	*	*	*							*	*		*	*
Russian Sage						*	*			*	*			*
Sandwort	*							*	*	*		*		
Sedum	*	*	*		*			*		*	*	*	*	
Shasta Daisy	*				*					*	*		*	*
Snow-in-summer	*							*	*	*		*		
Soapwort	*	*	*						*	*	*	*	*	
Speedwell	*	*				*	*			*		*	*	
Sweet Woodruff	*							*	*	*		*	*	
Tansy	*	*	*		*		*			*		*	*	*
Thrift	*	*							*	*		*	*	
Thyme	*	*					*	*	*	*		*	*	
Vinca	*					*	*	*	*	*	*	*		
Violet	*			*	*	*	*		*	*		*		
Wall Rockcress	*	*							*			*		
Wild Ginger							*	*		*		*		
Yarrow	*	*	*	*	*					*	*	*	*	*

Quick Reference Chart

Hardy	Semi-hardy	Tender	Sun	Part Shade	Light Shade	Shade	Moist	Well Drained	Dry	Fertile	Average	Poor	Page Number	SPECIES by Common Name
	HARDINESS			LIGHT				SOIL CONDITIONS						
	*	*	*					*	*			*	256	Mullein
*			*					*		*	*		258	Oriental Poppy
	*				*	*	*	*		*	*	*	262	Pachysandra
	*	*	*	*				*	*	*			264	Pasque Flower
*			*	*			*	*		*			266	Peony
*	*		*	*			*	*		*			270	Phlox
*			*	*				*	*	*	*		274	Pincushion Flower
*	*		*		*			*	*	*	*	*	276	Pinks
	*		*	*				*	*		*	*	280	Potentilla
*			*	*			*	*		*	*		284	Primrose
	*	*	*	*			*	*		*			288	Red-hot Poker
	*		*				*	*		*	*		290	Rose-mallow
	*	*	*					*	*		*	*	294	Russian Sage
*	*		*		*			*			*	*	296	Sandwort
*			*	*				*			*		298	Sedum
	*	*	*	*			*	*		*			302	Shasta Daisy
*			*	*				*	*		*	*	304	Snow-in-summer
*			*					*			*	*	306	Soapwort
*			*	*			*	*			*		308	Speedwell
	*			*	*	*	*			*	*		310	Sweet Woodruff
*	*		*				*	*	*		*	*	312	Tansy
	*		*					*	*		*	*	314	Thrift
	*		*					*	*		*	*	316	Thyme
*	*			*	*	*		*		*	*	*	320	Vinca
*	*		*	*	*		*	*		*			322	Violet
*	*		*					*			*	*	324	Wall Rockcress
*	*			*	*	*	*		*	*	*		326	Wild Ginger
*			*					*	*		*	*	328	Yarrow

GLOSSARY

Acid soil: soil with a pH lower than 7.0

Alkaline soil: soil with a pH higher than 7.0

Basal leaves: leaves that form from the crown

Crown: the part of a plant at or just below soil level where the shoots join the roots

Cultivar: a cultivated plant variety with one or more distinct differences from the species, such as flower colour, leaf variegation or disease resistance

Damping off: fungal disease causing seedlings to rot at soil level and topple over

Deadhead: to remove spent flowers to maintain a neat appearance and encourage a longer blooming period

Disbud: to remove some flowerbuds to improve the size or quality of the remaining ones

Dormancy: a period of plant inactivity, usually during winter or unfavourable climatic conditions

Double flower: a flower with an unusually large number of petals, often caused by mutation of the stamens into petals

Genus: a category of biological classification between the species and family levels; the first word in a Latin name indicates the genus

Hardy: capable of surviving unfavourable conditions, such as cold weather

Humus: decomposed or decomposing organic material in the soil

Hybrid: a plant resulting from natural or human-induced cross-breeding between varieties, species or genera; the hybrid expresses features of each parent plant

Neutral soil: soil with a pH of 7.0

Node: the area on a stem from which a leaf or new shoot grows

Offset: the young plant that naturally sprouts around the base of the parent plant

pH: a measure of acidity or alkalinity (the lower the pH, the higher the acidity); the pH of soil influences availability of nutrients for plants

Rhizome: a food-storing stem that grows horizontally at or just below soil level, from which new shoots may emerge

Rootball: the root mass and surrounding soil of a container-grown plant or a plant dug out of the ground

Semi-hardy: a plant capable of surviving the climatic conditions of a given region if protected

Semi-double flower: a flower with petals that form two or three rings

Single flower: a flower with a single ring of typically four or five petals

Species: the original species from which cultivars and varieties are derived; the fundamental unit of biological classification

Subspecies (subsp.): a naturally occurring, regional form of a species, often isolated from other subspecies but still potentially interfertile with them

Taproot: a root system consisting of one main root with smaller roots branching from it

Tender: incapable of surviving the climatic conditions of a given region and requiring protection from frost or cold

True: describes the passing of desirable characteristics from the parent plant to seed-grown offspring; also called breeding true to type

Tuber: the thick section of a rhizome bearing nodes and buds

Variegation: foliage that has more than one colour, often patched or striped or bearing differently coloured leaf margins

Variety (var.): a naturally occurring variant of a species; below the level of subspecies in biological classification

INDEX